FAWLTY TOWERS

FULLY BOOKED

BAY
BOOKS

DEDICATION

To those much-missed pillars of Fawlty Towers' society,
Major Gowen (Ballard Berkeley) and Terry the Chef (Brian Hall).

North American Edition published 2003 by Bay Books
by arrangement with BBC Worldwide Ltd.
Bay Books is an imprint of Bay | SOMA Publishing,
444 DeHaro St. #130, San Francisco, CA 94107

First published 2001 by BBC Worldwide Ltd.,
80 Wood Lane, London W12 0TT

ISBN 1-57959-079-9
Library of Congress Cataloging-in-Publication data on file with the publisher

Picture credits: All photographs ©BBC with the exception of the following:

Sally George p.72
Rex Features p.109, p.112, p.122

For the British Edition
Commissioning Editor: Ben Dunn
Project Editors: Rebecca Kincaid and April Warman
Book Design: designsection and Peacock
Picture Research: Bea Thomas
Production Controller: Christopher Tinker

For the American Edition
Publisher: James Connolly
Editorial Director: Floyd Yearout
Production: Jeff Swenerton

The publishers would like to thank Joe Mahoney and Ross McGinley for their help in the preparation of this book.

Printed and bound in France by Imprimerie Pollina s.a. - n° L88928
Color separations by Radstock Reproductions, Midsomer Norton, Somerset
Distributed by Publishers Group West

FAWLTY TOWERS FULLY BOOKED

CONTENTS

INTRODUCTION

'When I first read the scripts of *Fawlty Towers* it was one of those rare
occasions when I laughed continuously and with mounting delight.
Its anarchic and totally individual flavour was and is unique.
Certainly they were a joy to direct and produce, and gave everybody
concerned with the production enormous satisfaction,
but, probably more to the point, we never stopped laughing
from the beginning until the final fade-down.'

John Howard Davies – Director/Producer, Fawlty Towers, *Series One*

INTRODUCTION

THERE were just two series of *Fawlty Towers* – six half-hour episodes in 1975 and a further six in 1979. (Many reference books wrongly claim that there were 13 episodes.) When it first hit our television screens, Harold Wilson was prime minister, the war in Vietnam was drawing to an end, and the number of people unemployed in Britain hit one million. Inflation soared to 27 per cent, London had snow in June, Arthur Ashe became the first black singles champion at Wimbledon, and Margaret Thatcher became the first female leader of a British political party.

In the world of entertainment, the top films of 1975 were Hollywood blockbusters: *One Flew Over the Cuckoo's Nest* with Jack Nicholson, and Steven Spielberg's shark thriller, *Jaws*. Queen's 'Bohemian Rhapsody' hit the top of the charts and Bruce Springsteen released his breakthrough album *Born To Run*. The most popular comedy series then running on British television were the perennial favourites *The Two Ronnies* on BBC and ITV's *Man About the House*, although *The Good Life* was about to knock them both off their perch. Meanwhile, Jimmy Saville was delighting a younger generation with the start of *Jim'll Fix It*. It was also the year that the cult police drama *The Sweeney* first came roaring onto our screens, and actor William Hartnell, television's first Doctor Who and the 'man the Daleks couldn't kill', died at the age of 67.

It is a testament to the continuing popularity of *Fawlty Towers* that more than a quarter of a century since its first appearance the show is as popular as ever, and has an army of fans who were not even born when the shows were first transmitted. It may have run for just six hours but the series ranks among the finest situation comedies ever produced. As the film director Ralph Thomas – the man behind the *Doctor...* comedies – once commented: 'You don't get diamonds the size of bricks.' *Fawlty Towers* is certainly the jewel in the BBC's comedy crown.

And it's not just the British public who rate it so highly. During the year 2000's millennium poll fever, the British Film Institute compiled a list of the top 100 television shows in British broadcasting history. For once both the critics and the viewers agreed. *Fawlty Towers* was, by an enormous majority, voted the number one British show of the 20th century. In fact, it easily beat landmark dramas like *Cathy Come Home* and *The Singing Detective*, long-running soap favourites *Coronation Street* and *EastEnders*, and, perhaps most tellingly, even out-distanced John Cleese's earlier comedy success, *Monty Python's Flying Circus*.

Now, here at last, is the complete history of this groundbreaking comedy classic. With exclusive reminiscences from the stars and production team, and over 150 full-colour pictures, many of which are being published for the first time, this book is the definitive companion to the best television show ever made.

So imagine it's opening time, order a shot of whisky and join the Major and his friends for a nostalgic look back to find out why *Fawlty Towers* is worth a five-star rating.

THE HISTORY OF
FAWLTY TOWERS

'I know this middle class taboo is absurd and that anger is human and natural, but people have to push me to the very edge before I go: I bottle it up. Humour is a social sanction against inflexible behaviour.'

John Cleese on Fawlty Towers *in a* Radio Times *interview published in September 1975*

TWENTY-FIVE years later, few writer/performers have come close to matching, let alone bettering, the brilliant scripts and acting played out in that notorious Torquay hotel. The first of the *Monty Python* generation to achieve public recognition, thanks to his satirical performances in *The Frost Report*, Cleese was also the first ex-*Python* to break into mainstream comedy and outshine his previous achievements. Keen to move on from the *Python* collective, it was in fact during those heady days of location filming that the inspiration for *Fawlty Towers* first took seed.

In the same *Radio Times* interview quoted above, Cleese said: 'I dislike humour I can't believe in. No matter how daft something becomes, it's got to be credible at the level it's offered and real to the characters involved in it.' Indeed, the basis for his greatest comedy success was extremely real, and can be traced back to Tuesday 12 May 1971 when the six *Python* lads were staying in the Torbay area during a block of filming. The team had been booked into an apparently quiet, respectable place called the Gleneagles Hotel. (Connoisseurs of *Fawlty Towers* will recognize Gleneagles as the hotel in the episode 'The Builders' where the residents are told to go for their meals during the construction work. For John Cleese this was simply an affectionate nod back to his inspirational stay.)

The owner of the Gleneagles Hotel, and the man now burdened with the dubious accolade 'the real Basil Fawlty', was one Donald Sinclair.

OPPOSITE: The 'real' *Fawlty Towers*: Wooburn Grange Country Club, Buckinghamshire – now sadly demolished.

Dismayed at the mild-mannered requests and slightly unorthodox behaviour of the *Monty Python* team, and greeting them with a disgruntled sigh, Sinclair's clear dislike for guests of any shape or size was revealed almost instantly. The late Graham Chapman was outraged by his rudeness, and in his memoirs, *A Liar's Autobiography vol.IV,* he described Sinclair as 'completely round the twist, off his chump, out of his tree'. To make matters worse for the tippling Python, Chapman 'found the hotel intensely disagreeable in that it was impossible to get a drink'. Cleese vividly recalls his writing partner being refused a brandy by the hotel proprietor and remembers, 'He was so extraordinarily rude. One day we were all at

ABOVE: The internationally influential *Monty Python* gang – Terry Jones, Eric Idle, John Cleese, Graham Chapman and Michael Palin – before their fateful stay in Torquay.

OPPOSITE: The ever-resourceful Polly (Connie Booth) desperately trying to keep *Fawlty Towers* running smoothly.

dinner and Terry Gilliam was eating as Americans do, cutting all the meat up, putting the knife to one side, picking up the fork in the right hand and spearing the portions of meat. Mr Sinclair walked past Terry eating his meal and he had this look of complete astonishment on his face. He said, "We don't eat like that in this country!" On another occasion Eric Idle had left his briefcase by the front door of the hotel because we'd had to rush for a cab and he'd forgotten it. In the evening when we all arrived back at the hotel Eric explained that he had left his briefcase that morning. Mr Sinclair said, "Yes, it's at the far side of the wall." Eric looked out of the main entrance where he

was pointing and there was the swimming pool. At the far side of the swimming pool was a wall, and Eric, in amazement, said, "What – you mean the other side of the wall?" "What?" said Sinclair, and Eric repeated, "The other side of the wall! Why did you put it there?" Sinclair said, "We thought it might be a bomb." By this stage Eric was livid and spluttered, "A bomb!" I shall never forget Sinclair's response. He just looked completely unfazed and muttered, "Well, we've had some staff problems." It was priceless.'

Not surprisingly, most of the *Python* team could not tolerate this eccentric treatment and

promptly decamped to the nearby Imperial Hotel the following day. John Cleese, however, remained – fascinated by 'the most wonderfully rude man I've ever met'. He even invited his actress wife, Connie Booth, to join him at the hotel to observe the owner's outrageous mistreatment of staff and guests. It would prove a very fruitful exercise, given that by 1975 John Cleese was describing Connie Booth as 'the best writing partner I could have ... we always laugh at the same things'.

But it was as a solo writer that Cleese first capitalized on the unforgettable encounter with Donald Sinclair. During his close association with the BBC and the *Monty Python* programmes, Cleese had been hired by London Weekend Television producer Humphrey Barclay to pen a batch of half-hour situation comedy scripts for his *Doctor at Large* series. With the Sinclair experience still fresh in his mind, Cleese wrote the episode 'No Ill Feeling' which aired on 30 May 1971. The show is highly redolent of *Fawlty Towers* and deals with the fresh-faced Dr Upton (Barry Evans) staying at a seedy hotel along with a joke-cracking bore (Roy Kinnear) and a trio of old ladies, the

forebears of Miss Tibbs and Miss Gatsby (Lucy Griffiths, Ailsa Grahame and Betty Hare). However, it is the henpecked, petulant and humourless hotel owner, Mr Clifford (Timothy Bateson), who is most suggestive of *Fawlty Towers*, displaying an embryonic Basil Fawlty

persona. Dr Upton's continual, accidental ringing of the reception bell gets the owner's goat almost immediately as he snaps, 'Now what is it?' Older, seedier and more dour than Basil Fawlty, the character of Mr Clifford clearly owes much to Donald Sinclair. Similarly, the bizarre

OPPOSITE: 'I've been trying to get through to the speaking clock ... well it's been engaged for ten minutes. How is this possible? My wife isn't talking to it.'

ABOVE: 'Sybil, I think, is much stronger and more independent than Basil — she could really function perfectly well if Basil buzzed off or fell under a bus.' *John Cleese*.

situations and domestic disharmony in the hotel simply scream *Fawlty Towers*. Clifford's nagging wife, a mutton-dressed-as-lamb character, is played with Sybil-like pleasantries by Eunice Black. Other familiar ingredients include over-inquisitive hotel guests, lengthy waits for meals, wonderful slices of black humour and vengeful put-downs.

While less tightly structured than *Fawlty Towers*, this *Doctor at Large* episode, directed by Alan Wallis, shows the basic format and

characters pretty much in place. It's hardly surprising that Humphrey Barclay told Cleese that there was series potential in the episode. Cleese, however, dismissed the notion, and the idea lay dormant for several years.

When Cleese finally left the *Monty Python* team after the third series was broadcast from October 1972, he had just one ambition: 'Once I'd finished with *Python*, all I knew was that I wanted to do something with Connie Booth.'

Married since February 1968, Cleese and

Booth had already appeared on screen together in *How to Irritate People* and various *Monty Python* shows. The BBC were extremely keen to sign up the former *Python* favourite for his own comedy series. As Cleese remembers: 'I didn't know what to do, but I went and talked to Jimmy Gilbert, who was the head of light entertainment at the BBC, and said, "I'd like to do something with Connie." He said, "Fine! You come back with an idea."' Cleese remembers telling Connie Booth that Gilbert wanted a pilot episode of something. 'We spent about 20 minutes deciding we couldn't do the obvious male versus female comedy – the sort

OPPOSITE: Co-writers and co-stars John Cleese and Connie Booth relax on set during a break from filming.

ABOVE: As a last resort to convince their guests that Sybil is ill in bed, Basil strikes a deal with Polly in 'The Anniversary'.

Basil lost for words in 'The Anniversary' as Sybil comes face to face with friends who think she's ill upstairs in bed.

of material Mike Nichols and Elaine May had pioneered and performed so brilliantly. Besides, in Britain, John Fortune and John Bird had already covered that sort of ground with Eleanor Bron.'

Then Cleese remembered the hotel in Torquay and the encouraging words of Humphrey Barclay after the *Doctor at Large*

episode. Resurrecting their shared memories of Gleneagles from 1971, Cleese and Booth set about planning a pilot half-hour dealing with an irascible hotel manager and the irritating punters who ruin his day by staying at his establishment. 'This extraordinary man was very, very big in my memory, and within a very short time we'd figured out that

[Torquay] was where we wanted to set the hotel. The interesting thing is nobody thought it was a good idea. All the expert advice we got was that it was going to be very claustrophobic in a hotel.'

The enduring popularity of *Fawlty Towers* is not a by-product of an overly nostalgic viewing nation. There are few series that 25 years after their first showings have audiences sighing, 'Oh, they don't make them like that any more.' While the success of *Fawlty Towers* was never guaranteed, it is well deserved. However, far from being embraced as a ground-breaking success, Cleese recalls that the pilot script was snubbed by many bigwigs at the BBC. 'There's a famous memo which the current head of light entertainment has on the wall of his office. It concerns the pilot and says, "This is a very boring situation and the script has nothing but very clichéd characters. I cannot see anything but a disaster if we go ahead with it." A great friend of mine, Iain Johnstone, heard three producers at the bar saying, "Oh dear, have you seen this new script Cleese has done? Oh, it's terrible. Why did he ever leave *Monty Python?*" It's fascinating that when you try and do something new, nobody knows whether it's going to work or not.'

One person who was convinced it would work was the TV producer John Howard Davies, a former child actor best known for playing Oliver Twist in David Lean's 1948 film, and the eponymous hero in the 1951 *Tom Brown's Schooldays*. His comedy credentials were excellent: he had worked on the Derek Nimmo situation comedy *All Gas and Gaiters* and, most crucially, produced the first series of *Monty Python's Flying Circus* in 1969: 'When the first *Fawlty Towers* script came to me, courtesy of Jimmy Gilbert, I was a producer in the comedy department of the BBC. I fell out of bed laughing and was subsequently banned from reading the script at home. It was just so good, I couldn't understand how the script unit had not thought much of it.' Davies even suggests that Humphrey Barclay of London Weekend Television (LWT), the original champion of the idea, had been instrumental in allowing the BBC to make the programme, remembering that 'it had been turned down by LWT, who John had originally sent it to'. Jimmy Gilbert turned to Davies for advice. 'I said, "I think it's wonderful," and he countered, "It will only be wonderful if John Cleese does it, won't it?" I said, "Nobody else could possibly play it in a lifetime!" But at that stage we weren't absolutely sure that John wanted to play Basil Fawlty.'

Basil and Sybil, two names united in British comedy legend, were actually suggested to Cleese and Booth by Julian Doyle, the *Monty Python* film editor. Doyle was acquainted with a couple named Basil and Sybil, who were members of his local Communist Party.

As Cleese remembers, the writing duties were initially split 50:50 and according to gender: 'At the beginning I wrote most of Basil and most of Manuel, and Connie wrote most of Sybil and most of Polly. I found it very interesting because I'd sometimes suggest lines for Sybil, and Connie would say, "Oh no, no, a woman would never say that." Gradually, Connie started to write more Basil and I wrote more Sybil, and we co-operated more and more on all the characters.'

Prunella Scales, although nothing like the character of Sybil Fawlty as written, was delighted to land the part of the overbearing wife. Her first concern was with the motivation behind her character. Basil and Sybil seemed so unsuited that as an actress who likes to bring truth to her roles, she was troubled. 'The director John Howard Davies suggested me for the role, and I went along to see him in his flat. He was ill in bed with flu. He asked if there was anything I wanted to know about the script and I said, "Yes. Why did they ever get married?" He put the pillow over his head and exclaimed, "Oh, I was afraid you were going to ask that."

'I think it was my idea that she should be a little less posh than him, because otherwise what would have attracted them to each other? I had a vision of her family being in catering on the south coast or somewhere, and Sybil working behind a bar. I imagined Basil being demobbed from national service, receiving his gratuity, and then one evening going in for a drink where this barmaid fancied him because he was so posh. They both decide to get married and run a hotel together. Very romantic and idealistic. The grim reality then catches up with them.'

John Cleese remembers the questions he was asked about Basil and Sybil's marriage: 'When we handed in the first script there were a lot of theoretical questions about why are they together? I remember being puzzled by that. I said to the producer, "Look at all your friends. Do you have any idea why any of them are together?" And he said, "No, I suppose not." Sybil, I think, is much stronger and more independent than Basil – she could really function perfectly well if Basil buzzed off or fell under a bus. I don't think Basil could. He's very much more dependent on Sybil, and that's why he's much more frightened of her than she is of him.'

The character of Polly was fashioned as an ever-reliable confidante to the neurotic hotel owner. The writers had little trouble getting her character right, and John Howard Davies recalls: 'Connie's understanding of structure in the scripts was absolutely vital. And she acted as a very good yardstick from stopping us going too far and bringing a sensibility, a rationale and a logic to everything. As well as being delightfully intelligent, with a very good sense of humour and, probably most important of all, great legs.'

Polly may have been the easier of the characters to work out, but that didn't stop the writers changing their minds as to her aspirations. During the filming of the pilot episode they became unhappy with her character's status as a supposed philosophy student. They realized that Polly would work better as an art student and so several minutes of the show were subsequently re-recorded and re-edited before the first episode was transmitted to the general public.

Manuel was the last of the major characters to be slotted into place. From the start, John Cleese knew exactly who he wanted for the part, as John Howard Davies recalls: '... the brilliant and wonderful Andrew Sachs. Both John and I had seen him in a play called *No Sex Please, We're British*, and he was remarkable. He was wonderful and so acrobatic – he was such an obvious choice for the character ...absolutely right from the word go. We naturally rehearsed very hard for the first episode, but as soon as Andrew opened the script, he was Manuel.'

Sachs himself was delighted at the opportunity

of playing the character: 'My first impression was the role was very nice but I had to buckle down to the Spanish. I practised the accent on the way to the studios each day.' Sachs also contributed a minor, but intrinsic, part of the Manuel look: 'It was me who actually came up with the idea of a moustache for Manuel. I had never been a regular on TV, and I thought if I do suddenly become one, people will start recognizing me and I'll get

an image. I didn't think the producer would let me have one because John already had a moustache. Surprisingly, John Howard Davies agreed and it worked as a disguise. That was nice.'

On first seeing *Fawlty Towers*, some people within the business believed they knew the root of the emotional, sometimes violent, relationship between Basil and Manuel. Many claimed that Basil was pure John Cleese and Manuel was a milder, know-your-place version of fellow Python, Terry Jones. The heated debates between the two actors while working on *Monty Python* sketches had become legendary and often resulted in 'flying furniture'.

Cleese has vehemently denied any connection between his friend Jones and the character of Manuel. 'Besides,' he laughs, 'Terry's Welsh, and, as far as I know, Manuel isn't from the valleys.'

The inspiration for the loveable Major, however, is more cut and dried. He is a rose-

tinted version of Cleese's Latin teacher at prep school, the indomitable Captain Lancaster, whose overplayed readings of *Three Men in a Boat* had his junior audience convulsed with laughter.

ABOVE: 'Burro' – Basil gets to grips with a little more Spanish as he scolds Manuel for being too generous with the butter.

OPPOSITE: To kill time during the food emergency in 'Gourmet Night', Manuel entertains the Halls (Allan Cuthbertson and Ann Way) as Polly looks on.

Ballard Berkeley, who had enjoyed a long and varied acting career, was cast as the bemused military buffer and was perfect for the role.

The actors in place, it was time to put them through their paces.

Many of the basic ingredients of *Fawlty Towers*, such as lots of people running about shouting and screaming, often falling down,

and throwing or spilling things on each other, are essentially slapstick, but the wit of the writing, and the intricacy of the plotting make it actually pure farce. Though cream pies could feature largely in an episode, and Derek Royle, as the infamous 'corpse', got whisked around the building at high speed, *Fawlty Towers* was planned so as to make such slapstick-type

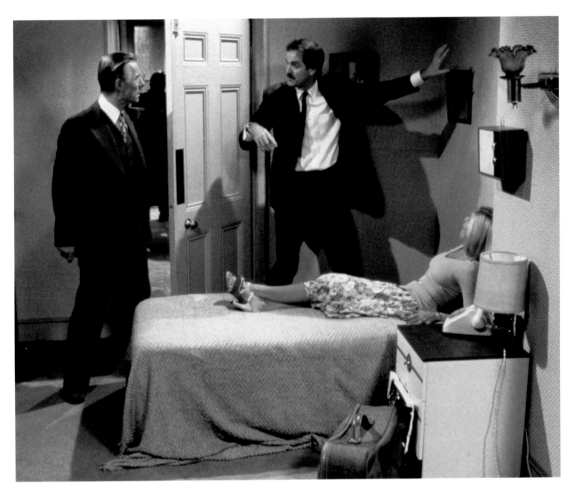

moments merely part of a tightly plotted, intense and emotional performance. John Cleese explains: 'I've always had a tremendous love for farce because what I like to do more than anything else is to really laugh. The essence of farce is almost always that some kind of taboo has been transgressed and the protagonist has to cover up. So he does one lie to cover up the first. As he seems to get caught out in that lie, he has to switch to a slightly different lie and then to a third until you just get bogged down in worse and worse degrees of lying.

'The thing is that everything has to happen in an exaggerated way. So although you may start it quite low key and quite real, it kind of winds up, and people get more and more frantic, trying to keep the frantic feelings in and present some sort

OPPOSITE: Basil, Polly and Manuel in hot pursuit of the laundry van in the frantic climax to 'The Kipper and the Corpse'.

ABOVE: Basil tries to explain the situation to Dr Abbott (Basil Henson) and Raylene Miles (Luan Peters) in 'The Psychiatrist'.

of calm façade to someone they have to impress. What I love is the intensity and the emotion because with that comes more frantic behaviour, more energy and the possibility of huge laughs.

'What a lot of people haven't spotted is that *Fawlty Towers* is just little 30-minute farces that start very, very low key and finish up absolutely frantic.'

Though the shows are so short, they aren't less involved than, say, a full-length feature film or stage play. If anything, they are more so, for three reasons. First, leaving aside the pilot episodes, half-hour shows are usually like the last two acts of a traditional three-act play in that the audience is already aware of the main characters, their setting and their relationship with each other. While that certainly makes it easier to develop running gags from one show to another, it also requires more ingenuity to squeeze laughter from what can become a well-worn situation. There's a fine line to tread in being successful in the former without

falling foul of the latter.

Second, the action has to build to a climax in a much shorter space of time than a film or stage play. Third, and perhaps most important, the programmes are viewed on a small screen, which reduces everything, so you have to ensure that the camerawork covers all angles, and the editing is as tight as possible so the viewer at home gets to see the farce unfold in a clear and logical fashion. Most half-hour sitcoms have about 65 pages of script and an average of 200 different camera cuts and angles per show. *Fawlty Towers*, however, had around 140 pages of script and 400 camera cuts and angles per episode. The technical demands meant that not one word of script could be written until the plot had been worked out first.

John Cleese is proud of his and Connie Booth's discipline in plotting their series: 'The shows were very well constructed, and what we discovered was that we never started to write the dialogue until we got the plot worked out.

We would spend sometimes as much as two and a half weeks on a plot. Not always the same one because if we got stuck on one, we'd sometimes put it to one side and pick up another that we were halfway through and try and run with that.'

Cleese and Booth would focus each show on one key idea – such as the visit of a health inspector or a guest dying on the premises – and run a couple of subplots beside it, the idea being that they would run in parallel for a time and then become entwined for the last five minutes, when all hell would break loose. For example, the key idea in 'Communication Problems' is a visit to the hotel by the

OPPOSITE: Communication problems: Basil and Mrs Richards (Joan Sanderson) at loggerheads.

RIGHT: The strain of dealing with this troublesome guest begins to show.

horrendous half-deaf harridan Mrs Richards, who makes life hell for those around her as she complains constantly in a bid to save herself money. The main subplot is that Basil, behind his wife's back, has acted on a racing tip from a guest and won himself a large sum of money which he wants to keep secret from the overbearing Sybil. Other threads include Polly being short of money and then having to explain to Sybil why she has a pile of cash (she is, in fact, holding on to it for Basil), and Mrs Richards thinking she has had some money stolen from her room. The threads come together when Sybil finds that Basil has been lying and Polly's money is his gambling win. Mrs Richards hasn't had any money stolen – she left it in her gloves when she went to buy a vase. The climax sees Basil accidentally break the vase and Sybil hand over his winnings to Mrs Richards to pay for the damage.

Cleese says: 'Some people try to write comedy by starting at scene one and writing the dialogue. The chances of them getting to a satisfactory ending are one in a hundred. You've got to know where you're going while you're building the thing. Connie and I were literally there sitting next to each other all the time that it was written. I think I learnt a lot about the process of writing – mainly that some days it flows and other days it doesn't – and that you mustn't become too despairing on the days when it doesn't work because a good day will be coming up. Although you can never tell which is which, you can kind of average it that over a week you'll probably have three days when it's flowing well and two days when it isn't. And that enables you to relax because

when you have the bad day you think, "Maybe we'll have a good day tomorrow."'

Once it came to making the show, Cleese was a formidable taskmaster, a perfectionist in writing and in the studio. Rehearsal schedules were tight and there was much to learn. The cast and crew had just five days to get it right. When the actors arrived at 9 a.m. on the Wednesday morning, they were expected to have all their lines memorized. As Prunella Scales recalls: 'I can't say that it was an idyllically happy time because it was such hard work that you don't have time to

In a desperate attempt to catch him out, Basil checks up on the laid-back Mr Johnson (Nicky Henson) in 'The Psychiatrist'.

think if you were happy or not. It was a question of getting the lines learnt by Wednesday morning and rehearsing your knickers off until we actually recorded it on Sunday night. Very, very, very hard graft. John was extremely rigorous and used every second of rehearsal time and he was quite cross on Wednesday morning if you didn't know it perfectly ... and quite rightly too.'

As well as producing the first series of *Fawlty Towers*, John Howard Davies also directed it. Although a relative newcomer to the world of television direction, he was aware that turning the scripts into first-class shows would take a good deal of work from all concerned: 'We had a lot of fun at the read-through stage — just getting everyone together round a table ... and reading it through for the first time. Then we went straight into rehearsal and blocked it all out in movement terms. After about the second day most people knew everything by heart. Sometimes there were fluffs, but I found that after three days' rehearsal I could remember the script by heart too without consciously learning it. John was wonderful with his lines ... because he and Connie had written it, after all. Even so, the sheer speed in which we rehearsed was incredible. We could laugh an awful lot, but we worked very, very hard at it to get it right.'

Cleese, his cast and particularly the crew soon found that five days per show in a studio was a punishing schedule. By the time the show came to be recorded on the Sunday evening most of them were exhausted. And if they thought they would get a break in the hours leading up to the recording, they were mistaken. John Howard Davies points out: 'We used to record between eight and nine-thirty on Sunday nights — always on Sunday nights — and I used to make everybody do two runs in the afternoon — the first one was to try absolutely everything out to see if it worked, and the second was just a sort of walk-through.'

The schedule may have been exhausting, but everyone felt they were part of the process and the writers were more than happy to have ideas from the cast members themselves, as Cleese recalls: 'It felt to me very much like a team effort because we all listened to each other a great deal. If I was doing a scene with Pru, then Connie and Andrew would just sit there watching, and after a time one of them might make a suggestion or say that they think something isn't quite working. Now because Connie and I had written and then rewritten the scripts, there wasn't an enormous amount of script rewriting — they were more or less right most of the time. But how we did them was very much a co-operative thing with lots of suggestions coming in.'

Filming of the shows took place mainly in BBC studios, though there were some scenes that had to be shot on location and added during the editing process at a later date. The occasion when Basil beats his car with a branch, for example, was filmed in Mentmore Close in Kenton, north London. The actual exteriors of *Fawlty Towers* weren't filmed in Torquay, but in Buckinghamshire at Wooburn Grange Country Club in Bourne End which doubled for the infamous hotel, and André's restaurant in the 'Gourmet Night' episode was actually 294 Preston Road in Harrow. John Howard Davies says that juggling the location footage presented subtle problems: 'What was immensely difficult was filming all the inserts weeks before we did the series and then slotting them in, ensuring we got the right pace for the shows that were subsequently recorded in the studio. It really wasn't easy.'

John Cleese and Connie Booth were the first to admit that the opening batch of episodes was written as much for their own pleasure as for calculated TV success. Indeed, it seemed at first that *Fawlty Towers* was going to be one of those comedy series loved more by people within the industry than those outside it. Cleese says, 'My experience has always been that if you do something that is original, it takes a little time for any kind of momentum to build up. We had no idea that it was going to have the impact that it did. I always assumed it might pick up half the *Monty Python* audience, which itself wasn't huge. *Fawlty Towers* was a comedy of emotion and more people were able to plug into it.'

While *Fawlty Towers* won the British Academy Award for Best Comedy Series of 1975, none of the episodes ever made it into the week's top 10 viewing figures. This might have had something to do with the lukewarm critical response from some areas of the media. As Cleese remembers, 'The *Daily Mirror* said, "Long John, short on jokes" after the second episode, and one of the Edinburgh papers said it was very poor.

'And then there was a sort of a rumble of fairly positive reaction towards the end of the series. That's the time when the critics should take a show really seriously, about number four of the series, and not before then. Of course, most don't realize this because although some are able to say whether something is good or bad, very few understand the process of comedy.'

The BBC obviously had more faith in its production than the critics, and within weeks of the first series coming to an end, promptly repeated all six episodes during January and February 1976. Following close on the heels of his BAFTA victory, John Cleese received the 1976 Royal Television Society Programme Award for outstanding creative achievement for his work on *Fawlty Towers* – no mean feat for a man aged just 36.

Cleese toyed with the idea of capitalizing on the series' success and opening a restaurant in partnership with his friend, restaurateur Andrew Leeman, who would provide the inspiration for 'The Kipper and the Corpse'. A Knightsbridge location was found for the restaurant provisionally named Basil's, but the scheme was abandoned.

In light of the show's burgeoning popularity, it would have seemed reasonable for the BBC to rush a second series into production. This didn't happen, primarily because John Cleese and Connie Booth were at a loss as to how to develop the show and its themes without diluting the multi-layered and tightly structured humour. Cleese says: 'The problem we had with a second series of *Fawlty Towers* was that the expectation was unreasonably high. I realized that people were already remembering the first series as better than it was. There were three or four things in the first series that were really funny and the audience remembered those as the general standard rather than the highlights. They would have expected the second series to be at the highlight level all the way through.'

John Cleese and Connie Booth in rehearsal for 'The Anniversary'. Could it be that the newspaper headline is referring to the on-set fight (see page 39) that delayed the episode's filming and broadcast by a week?

The BBC knew they had a long-term hit on their hands, and they continued to cajole Cleese and Booth into writing further instalments. The pair were not ready to commit to a further series, and even the mooted idea of one-off seasonal specials came to nothing.

The most important reason for the *Fawlty Towers* well drying up – if only temporarily –

was that the marriage of John Cleese and Connie Booth was coming to an end. The couple divorced during 1976, and a difficult time was made none the easier by speculation that the pressures of writing the series had caused the split. Cleese dismisses this: 'We split up between the first and the second series. I don't think that show business was anything

ABOVE: Una Stubbs and the original Roger, Julian Holloway, in rehearsal for 'The Anniversary'…

OPPOSITE: … and the final Roger, Ken Campbell, with Una Stubbs and John Cleese.

to do with the fact that we separated, though a lot of people thought it was. It was the right decision and, oddly enough, the time we spent together we both view very positively. As Tom Stoppard said, all relationships have a clock attached to them.'

Ironically, it was soon after their marriage break-up that the couple came together again and decided to work on a second series of *Fawlty Towers*. In an effort to ensure that the second batch of programmes was not just as good as the first series, but better, the two threw themselves into a rigorous, long and demanding schedule, taking over a month to

pen a single episode. This meant that series two took up to a year in its various pre-production stages – something of a feat in studio-recorded television comedy circles. Cleese admits that they pushed themselves to the limit: 'We found the second series so demanding. We felt that the audience was getting to know the characters so well that they'd get to the point of the joke before us. Connie and I found it was probably as difficult as anything we'd done because the hardest thing in this business is to deal with real expectations. It was a huge effort to get those scripts as good as I think they finally were. About six weeks each. So that's about 36 weeks' writing. Then there was one week of location filming and one week per episode in the studio – a 43-week shoot, for which I was paid the princely sum of £9000. Not quite retirement money, but there were repeats.'

Comedy veteran Douglas Argent, who had produced the final episodes of *Steptoe and Son*, and director Bob Spiers, who went on to make the last series of *The Goodies*, *Spice World: The Movie* and *Absolutely Fabulous*, were put in charge of production. Finally, after more than three years, the BBC got their second series of *Fawlty Towers*.

Bob Spiers remembers his nervousness at taking over the directing helm: 'The reason I got this job was down to John Howard Davies who had directed and produced the first series and who had become head of light entertainment. He asked what show I'd like to direct. Just off the top of my head I said *Fawlty Towers*. And two weeks later he very, very, very kindly gave it to me.

'It was a bit nerve-racking because I was relatively inexperienced. In fact, I'd only

directed a couple of shows on my own – *It Ain't Half Hot Mum* was my first. Apart from that I used to direct dance routines for *Seaside Special* on Brighton beach, as inserts for a variety show that used to go out on Saturday night. So this was a big, big, big programme for me to be doing.'

Bob Spiers directed his cast and crew through six episodes, which were broadcast from February 1979. An unfortunate incident during production of the fifth episode, however, nearly made everything come unstuck. Cleese remembers: 'We got about five days into rehearsal and a splendid thing happened. A BBC executive got into an argument with a technician – a rigger, I think – and eventually punched him. The unions went on strike and we couldn't record the programme on the originally scheduled day. As a result, the recording was postponed, and although the strike was settled and the programme was filmed the following week, we lost one of the cast. Julian Holloway was unable to do the second week because he had another commitment, so we brought in dear Ken Campbell, who's such a marvellous, strange and funny man.'

As if that wasn't enough, production of the final episode, 'Basil the Rat', was also affected. Britain had been grinning and bearing it over the past few months as the infamous 'winter of discontent' took its icy grip on the nation's services. Corpses weren't being buried, rubbish was building up in the streets and the rail network was even worse than usual. The unions had pitted themselves against a collapsing Labour government. By the time 1979 arrived, it was obvious that Prime Minister James

Callaghan was going to call an election some time during the spring or early summer. The strikes continued and even affected television broadcasting. By late March, parts of the BBC were on strike. This led to a delay of several weeks in filming the last episode, which consequently missed its allotted broadcast slot.

The final episode of *Fawlty Towers* was eventually transmitted some six months after its original time slot, on 25 October 1979. This

ABOVE: John Cleese and Prunella Scales in rehearsal at the reception desk that has seen everything from garden gnomes to moose heads.

OPPOSITE: Basil tries to dissuade Alice (Una Stubbs) from going upstairs to see his 'ill' wife in 'The Anniversary'.

turned out to be something of a blessing in disguise, for by the time the show aired, the ITV network had itself come out on strike and for 10 weeks during the summer and early autumn all commercial broadcasting was halted. This meant that the public had only two channels from which to choose their daily viewing. All BBC programmes suddenly found themselves with record-breaking audiences.

From a production point of view, director Bob Spiers was quite pleased by the enforced delay on the last episode of the series: 'It actually worked to our advantage. After the initial read-through, I'd analysed what was involved in this episode in terms of special effects and rats running around all over the place, and the number of scenes we had to do. In my opinion, it was totally impossible to do it with just one day in the studio; it was too complex to achieve in one hit. It just would never ever have worked. Luckily, with this little delay, I was able to go cap in hand to the powers that be and they very grudgingly agreed to allow me two days in the studios and some pre-record time for the special effects.'

Transmitting the final *Fawlty Towers* episode during the ITV strike gained the show a much wider audience than it had previously enjoyed, and was responsible for a Christmas repeat of 'The Psychiatrist' winning the series its first top 10 position in the chart of viewing figures. Spiers acknowledges the connection: 'There was just a funny feeling when I was editing 'Basil the Rat' that the series had gone really well up to that point, and I had a kind of sense that this episode was going to be a ... bit special. Of course with the delay, the great British public were just waiting to see this particular one. It was a very exciting time. We had the confidence, with the other shows having gone out and being so well received, that we were doing something right.'

That view was corroborated when the series was voted best comedy at that year's BAFTA ceremony. Internationally, too, *Fawlty Towers* was clearly something of a major BBC export, but there was a surprise in store at the Montreux Television Festival. The BBC chose 'The Kipper and the Corpse' as its entry and it was widely tipped to win the gold award. Amazingly, it won nothing at all. Many of the international judges, it seemed, were appalled at the stock comic characterization of Manuel as a stereotypical funny foreigner.

John Cleese, however, got the last laugh – twice. First, a short film, *To Norway, Home of Giants*, which he had written and narrated for the Norwegian entry under the pseudonym of Norman Fearless, won two prizes at the festival. Even sweeter was the news that *Fawlty Towers* was fast becoming the biggest-selling success in the BBC's history. During 1977 and 1978 alone the first series had been sold to some 45 television stations in 17 different countries. All the audiences, including the Germans, relished the six programmes, and in Spain, where the Manuel character could have caused confusion, the waiter's nationality was changed to Italian.

Another important development in the success of *Fawlty Towers* occurred in 1979 when the BBC released selected soundtracks of the shows as records.

John Howard Davies, the producer/director of the first series, remembers those recordings: 'After six months of trying I finally persuaded BBC Enterprises, the sales arm of the BBC, to make a vinyl LP record of *Fawlty Towers*. I thought it might sell rather well. They didn't think so. They told me that they thought it was a very bad idea and didn't believe it would sell at all. Eventually they decided they'd do it and radio producer John Lloyd produced it. The record made about £100,000. I rather plaintively rang up and said could I have a little bit of money too please because it was my idea. Their answer was for me to write the record sleeve [notes] which would give them an

OPPOSITE: Polly, Manuel and Basil unite in bidding a fond farewell to another dissatisfied guest.

Basil typing up the menu at the beginning of the pilot episode 'A Touch of Class'.

excuse to pay me. I eventually got a cheque for £25, which I still have framed.'

The first record, which presented 'Communication Problems' (renamed 'Mrs Richards' for the disc) and 'The Hotel Inspectors', proved hugely popular and remains something of a collector's item. The linking narration was written and performed by Andrew Sachs in the character of Manuel, a necessity to explain any visual business lost on sound-only recordings. A further record, featuring 'Basil the Rat' and 'The Builders', was produced in 1981. That same year saw the release of *We Are Most Amused*, a collection of classic comedy moments, including a brief interlude from the *Fawlty Towers* episode 'The Hotel Inspectors', in aid of the Prince's Trust. The third and final BBC record, released in 1982, presented 'The Kipper and the Corpse' (renamed 'Death' for the record) and 'The Germans' (retitled 'Fire Drill'). Although no more records were issued, the BBC released all 12 programmes on cassette as part of their Audio Collection range.

Given the enormous popularity of *Fawlty Towers*, the BBC were understandably keen to prolong the series. After all, a mere 12 episodes of such a winning format was hardly saturation point as far as they were concerned. It was the end, however, for John Cleese and Connie Booth. Both felt that while the second series was even better than the first, to try to top the second with an even better third series was a near impossibility. In the end, both realized that if more *Fawlty Towers* was to appear, the format would have to be bigger, and that meant feature films.

The tradition of TV sitcoms transferring to the big screen had been a long and mainly successful one. Hammer Films initiated the idea when they filmed the ITV favourite *The Army Game* as *I Only Arsked!* in 1959. It was Hammer again that fully relaunched the notion with its 1971 blockbuster *On the Buses*, which remains to this day the company's biggest home market financial success. Two *Buses* sequels followed as well as *Man About the House*, *Rising Damp* and *George and Mildred*. BBC classics like *Steptoe and Son*, *Dad's Army*, *Porridge* and *Are You Being Served?* had all gone on to be successful films. Cleese and Booth, however, didn't want a straight transfer – they wanted 'something completely different'. Their plan involved removing the hotel completely and utilizing the characters in a broader, more ambitious landscape. Cleese remembers: 'We had an idea for a plot which I loved. Basil was finally invited to Spain to meet Manuel's family. He gets to Heathrow and then spends about 14 frustrating hours waiting for the flight. Finally, on the plane, a terrorist pulls a gun and tries to hijack the thing. Basil is so angry he overcomes the terrorist and when the pilot says, "We have to fly back to Heathrow," Basil says, "No, fly us to Spain or I'll shoot you." He arrives in Spain, is immediately arrested and spends the entire holiday in a Spanish jail. He is released just in time to go back on the plane with Sybil. It was very funny but I couldn't do it at the time. Making *Fawlty Towers* work at 90 minutes was a very difficult proposition. You can build the comedy up for 30 minutes, but at that length there has to be a trough and another peak. It doesn't interest me. I don't want to do it.'

An earlier idea had Basil making the trip to Spain and staying in a crummy hotel owned by a Spaniard even ruder than himself. In the end, of course, all notions of a feature film and, indeed, any resurrection of the Basil Fawlty character at all were shelved. As Cleese comments: 'We'd got six hours out of Basil, which wasn't bad. Shakespeare only got three and a half from Hamlet, and look how he's lasted.'

In fact, Basil has endured in the most surprising of places. In April 1982, a full decade since John Cleese had founded the instructional film company Video Arts, the use of two episodes of *Fawlty Towers* for training purposes won a Queens Award for Export Achievement. The Hyatt hotel chain had used selected *Fawlty Towers* episodes as a business tool, while 'Gourmet Night' was hired out to the London Hilton and British Holiday Inns for staff training, showing them what not to do in a catering crisis. 'It didn't surprise me,' says Cleese. 'I'd already done countless videos about customer relations, and I had a good idea how you were really supposed to treat customers. It was very simple doing the opposite, as Basil. I just had to know the rule and break it.'

Constant rumours that *Fawlty Towers* was on the way back were always vastly exaggerated. As far as John Cleese and Connie Booth were concerned, they had been there and done that. The show was very much in the past. Other film-makers and television executives were, however, more than keen to revive memories of the series. In 1981 Cleese found himself as a guest star in *The Great Muppet Caper* alongside Joan Sanderson, who had played Mrs Richards. Three years later Cleese was delighted to be offered a role in a prestigious mini-series about the life of the composer Richard Wagner, but was dismayed to find that his part was nothing more than a pseudo-Basil Fawlty rant. He informed the producers that the cameo was not for him, and the desperate executives made the situation even worse by assuring Cleese that they were going to cast Prunella Scales in the role of his wife. However, Cleese was happily reunited with Andrew Sachs and Prunella Scales for various Video Art films and Amnesty charity performances. Indeed, as late as 2000, Scales joined Cleese in a number of self-contained comedy sketches for the BBC series *The Human Face*. They weren't playing Basil and Sybil, but the connotations were clear. Even the hugely popular Tesco commercials, starring Scales, were studied in parallel with the ill-fated Sainsbury's campaign headed by Cleese, by zealous journalists. To both the public and the media, Cleese and Scales are bound as tightly as the characters they created.

Fawlty Towers is regularly repeated on television, its familiarity seeming only to breed even fonder memories. In fact, the repeat to mark its 10th anniversary (in November 1985) attracted a staggering audience of 12.5 million – the record for BBC2. High-profile fans include the distinguished film directors Martin Scorsese and Bertrand Tavernier, and in 1991, when the Gulf War was raging, President George Bush reputedly relaxed during the conflict by watching episodes of the series.

Like *Monty Python's Flying Circus*, *Fawlty Towers* cracked both the European and the US markets. Interestingly, an Americanized version of *Fawlty Towers* (entitled *Snavely*), starring Harvey Korman and Betty White in the Basil and Sybil roles, was a disaster. John Cleese, talking soon after the programme was abandoned, believed that 'the producers feared it was too mean-spirited', noting that the American sitcom tradition is to have redeeming traits in every character. 'There was a noticeable attempt to reassure the audience that the people in the show were all right folks.'

Worse was to come. In 1983, another attempt was made to transport the essence of *Fawlty Towers* across the Atlantic. The result was a six-part series called *Amanda's by the Sea*, starring future Golden Girl Bea Arthur. Amazingly, the Basil Fawlty character was completely written out of the series. Disgusted, Cleese removed his name from the credit. A later American series, *Newhart*, starring Bob Newhart as writer turned innkeeper Dick Loudon, has often been cited as a *Fawlty Towers* remake, but none of the 184 episodes were based on anything like the Fawlty tradition or situation.

The latest US attempt to remake *Fawlty Towers* occurred with CBS in 1998, when John Cleese and Connie Booth signed over the format rights to the scripts and the characters but not the title. Called *Payne*, it stars John Larroquette and JoBeth Williams as the owners of Whispering Pines, a renovated Victorian inn in northern California. The bellhop Mo (played by Rick Batalla) and chambermaid Breeze O'Rourke (Julie Benz) are clearly Manuel and Polly stateside. Poor viewing figures led to only

nine episodes being made but Cleese was impressed with the results: 'I've only seen one episode of *Payne* and I thought what was smart was they tried to get away from doing *Fawlty Towers* the way we've done it. There was absolutely no point in reproducing what had already been done, so they're trying to make it something of their own. Don't forget, *Fawlty Towers* is only ever seen by the PBS audience, which is two to three per cent of the people who watch television in America. That means that 97 per cent of the people have never seen it, so they then enjoy the new series.'

The latest plans for redevelopment came in 2000 from perhaps the most unlikely place – Germany. The shows had first been broadcast in the country on cable television during 1993, and proved a tremendous success. A spokesman for the TV company said: 'German audiences were most keen on the slapstick elements, especially the violence shown by Basil towards Manuel. The "don't mention the war" scene did not cause offence.' However, when the series was remade for German television in 2001, 'The Germans' episode was jettisoned.

Fawlty Towers is clearly enjoyed worldwide and no one is more surprised than John Cleese himself: 'I've seen myself in Japanese and it's incomprehensible to me how this stuff translates, but it must.' Miami once held a Basil Fawlty Festival, and a journalist on New York's *Newsday* started a campaign for Basil Fawlty to be elected British prime minister. In a mock election, Basil won 63 per cent of the vote. Basil, Manuel and Sybil lookalikes do a roaring trade at parties, social functions and conferences. Indeed, hotels named *Fawlty Towers* have sprung up all over, from Florida and Western Australia to Zambia and Belgium. The ultimate replica was in Sidmouth, Devon, where the owner, one Stuart Hughes, changed his name to Basil Fawlty by deed poll in 1985 and promptly got himself elected as a member of the East Devon District Council representing the Monster Raving Loony Green Giant People's Party. Torquay, ironically, seems to be one of the few places that hasn't got its own *Fawlty Towers*.

The Gleneagles Hotel, from which John Cleese drew his inspiration in 1971, still stands. And the original owner, Donald Sinclair, is reputed to haunt the premises ... still refusing to leave his hated customers alone.

REGULARS

JOHN CLEESE
BASIL FAWLTY

'Connie and I saw Basil as someone who was tremendously class-conscious, who was always trying to become a little bit grand.'

John Cleese

IN Basil Fawlty, John Cleese, as both performer and co-writer, created the most enduring and endearing ogre in the history of the sitcom. Cleese comments: 'Connie and I saw Basil as someone who was tremendously class-conscious, who was always trying to become a little bit grand. He adopted attitudes of superiority over people that were really quite unjustified. And he was someone who was fundamentally terrified of his wife. If you look at the episodes, they're almost all fuelled by the fact that he is trying to hide something from Sybil. It's very, very basic.'

With the pomposity of Captain Mainwaring, the gloom of Tony Hancock, the self-importance of Rigsby and the deviousness of Norman Stanley Fletcher, Fawlty seems to develop from and outshine all comparable characters. But what sets him at the top of the comedy league table is that unlike the other, character actor-driven, reality-based characters just mentioned, Fawlty has an alien attitude to the codes and conventions that surround him. He could be described as almost sociopathic, not fully aware of the reality of the people he's interacting with. He is thus able to act in bizarre and extreme ways, screeching 'Don't mention the war!' at people who would prefer to forget it, as his grip on normality becomes looser and looser. Inevitably, with Cleese's 10-year grounding in sketch comedy, there is a sense of 'anything goes' flamboyance. The character of Fawlty is straight out of a *Monty Python* skit, but has the additional strength of being a fully developed, three-dimensional character. The situations and personalities that populate his world are, in the main, fairly straight and realistic. It is the contrast between

their sanity and the battling, frantic, maelstrom of Basil that infuses the whole with hilarity.

Significantly, Cleese regards his role as writer as far more important than that of actor. For him, the actual business of 'doing the funnies' is fairly tedious, certainly secondary to the pleasure of pursuing bizarre scenarios to their logical and comical conclusions. In his ability to portray the nature of English eccentricity, to examine what makes the nation tick and, most crucially, to make us laugh uproariously, Cleese remains a master of comedy. Following in the illustrious footsteps of Spike Milligan and Peter Cook, who did so much to develop anarchic humour, Cleese looked into his own middle-class upbringing to recreate the repressed, self-righteous and opinionated psyche of the 'typical' British male.

John Marwood Cleese was born on 27 October 1939 in Weston-super-Mare and, as Cleese says, 'If you came from Weston-super-Mare, you didn't go into show business. You became an accountant or a lawyer or possibly sold insurance – there were no other possibilities.' Contrary to popular myth, Cleese didn't change his name from Cheese to pursue a show business career. It was his father who, understandably, made the change in order to avoid ridicule when he enlisted during the Second World War. With his parents relatively old when he was born – his father, Reginald, was 46, and his mother, Muriel, was 40 – the young John Cleese had a sheltered and comfortable childhood. In the quiet gentility of Weston, his first ambition was to have his own bicycle, but his mother's concern for safety meant that he never acquired one. Cambridge contemporaries such as Tim Brooke-Taylor and Bill Oddie recall the amusing spectacle of the towering student Cleese bitterly complaining that he never had his own Raleigh.

Even as a boy, comedy, particularly radio comedy, fired his imagination. His earliest favourites – Amos 'n' Andy, the Marx Brothers and Abbott and Costello – were from the cross-talking, fast-witted tradition of American vaudeville. In 1949, at the age of 10, Cleese discovered the spiralling comic monologues of the young Frankie Howerd, then making his name on BBC Radio's *Variety Band-Box*. Off from school and sick in bed, Cleese amused himself by writing page upon page of comic dialogue in his exercise books. The material was written in the bantering style of Jimmy Jewel and Ben Warris – another favourite duo, from the BBC Radio series *Up the Pole*.

'I was always fascinated by comedy,' admits Cleese. 'I can vividly remember using my school exercise books to write scripts in ... Every time I heard a good joke, I used to write it down in the margins, so I was certainly finding myself in comedy. I watched an enormous number of American sitcoms in the mid-50s, with people like George Burns and Gracie Allen, Jack Benny, Phil Silvers, Joan Davis.' Years later in *Fawlty Towers*, after a particularly detached comment from Ballard Berkeley's Major, Basil is heard to mutter, 'Say goodnight to the folks, Gracie,' a direct homage to the closing words of *The Burns and Allen Show*. Cleese believes that, 'In retrospect, it was almost as though I was studying them.'

Six foot tall by the age of 12, Cleese's ability to create comic put-downs proved a useful weapon against playground bullies during his early education at St Peter's Preparatory School in Weston. While there, he also made his first, rather tentative steps towards an acting career with a featured role in *A Cure for Colds*: 'I quite enjoyed it, although I was terribly scared in terms of stage fright.' Scornful of traditional Shakespearean acting technique, and often using the radio series *I'm Sorry I'll Read That Again* as an anti-Bard performance platform, Cleese struggled through the lead role in *Scenes from Twelfth Night: The Tricking of Malvolio*. (It may not have been until Jonathan Miller directed him in a late 1970s television adaptation of *The Taming of the Shrew* that Cleese fully saw the potential of acting in Shakespeare.) This interpretation of the cross-gartered love slave was greeted with admiration. Even as a pre-teen actor, Cleese could deliver his lines with skill (as his teachers and audience discovered).

In December 1951 Cleese's writing was rewarded when he won the 12-and-over writing competition at his prep school. In 1953 he moved on to Clifton College in Bristol, where he took A-levels in physics, maths and chemistry.

During his time at Clifton, Cleese played for the school football team, but it was cricket at which he excelled. It has remained an abiding passion and during the 1970s when *Fawlty Towers* was at its peak, he even found time to contribute to the Taverners charity publication, *The Sticky Wicket Book*, compiled by main players Tim Rice and Willie Rushton. It is sport that provides Cleese with his proudest memory. Unlike his claim in *The International*

Film and Television Year Book that his favourite memory is 'scoring England's winning goal in the 1966 World Cup final', his cricketing claim to fame is nearly as impressive and has the virtue of being true. While a member of Clifton College's First XI, Cleese played several public school matches on the hallowed turf at Lord's. In Cleese's last year at the college, the team played the mighty MCC and Cleese secured the wicket of the legendary Denis Compton: caught Whitty, bowled Cleese for 22.

Acting was still tugging at his attention, however, and during his days at Clifton, Cleese performed in Molière's *Tartuffe* and, perhaps more tellingly, adapted some Michael Flanders and Donald Swann-type material for the end-of-term revue. Like his future fellow Pythons and, indeed, almost anybody worth their salt in British comedy during the latter half of the 20th century, Cleese was transfixed by the bizarre genius of *The Goon Show*, and particularly admired the intricate madness of Spike Milligan. Peter Cook, the principal force behind *Beyond the Fringe*, Cambridge Footlights' most influential revue, was similarly inspired by the Goons, even faking illness in order to have time to listen to them.

Comedy, however, was never considered a career option for Cleese and his generation. Their academic backgrounds pointed to much more serious pursuits. His success at A-level sciences, and his passion for biology (he had a particular interest in B.F. Skinner's behavioural tests on rats) pointed to a career as a research scientist, but when he passed the entrance exams for Downing College, Cambridge, he chose to accept their offer of a place to study

law. This was deferred for two years because the abolition of National Service in 1957 resulted in a torrent of applications from around the country and the university simply couldn't take all the students. To pass the time, Cleese took up a teaching post at his old prep school.

Once at Cambridge, he was encouraged to audition for Footlights, the university's drama society. Admitting to a complete incompetence in both dance and song (he had been forced into taking extra Greek instead at school because of his lack of promise), he was asked by the president of the club what skills he could bring to the group. Cleese half-heartedly muttered: 'I suppose I try to make people laugh!' (He had been conspicuously successful in this at school, and one particularly vicious and accurate comment aimed at his headmaster caused one member of staff to fall off his chair with laughter.)

Although initially rejected by Footlights, Cleese eventually found a way through the back door. Having teamed up with Alan Hutchinson, a fellow student he had met on his second day at Cambridge, he co-wrote and performed sketches for his own amusement. Hutch, who had some influence with Footlights, eventually succeeded in getting Cleese admitted to the company. Cleese was delighted when one of their sketches – a surreal news report about a dog stuck down a mineshaft whose owners die in their attempts to rescue it – was used by the group in June 1961. It was performed by Humphrey Barclay (later a radio and television producer) in the revue called *I Thought I Saw It Move*. Other members of the cast included David Frost,

The almost full Monty: Terry Jones, Terry Gilliam, Michael Palin and John Cleese celebrate 30 years of *Monty Python* in October 1999.

Mike Burrell and John Wood, who would later change his name to John Fortune and become a vital part of the sixties satire movement, and who still remains at the cutting edge of British comedy with his work opposite John Bird and Rory Bremner. Cleese recalls: 'I found that I could make people laugh, but I still had no intention of going into show business. In those days, say 1962, 1963, people from Cambridge didn't think of doing it. Within three years, all the people who went to Cambridge were practically planning to go into show business if they had those kind of talents.'

Moving to university digs 300 yards from the law school and a mere 100 yards from the Footlights headquarters, Cleese fell in with a bunch of future comic talents that included Tim Brooke-Taylor and Bill Oddie. He continued to write sketches, and their acerbic wit was well received. And then Cleese met Graham Chapman.

Initially Cleese found the blond-haired, pipe-smoking, gin-drinking medical student rather odd, but a friendship soon sparked and the duo began writing sketches together. Their first collaboration was for the 1962 Footlights revue, *Double Take*: 'I thought it was terribly good, which it wasn't!' It did, however, prove popular enough to be taken to that year's Edinburgh festival although most of the participants – including Tim Brooke-Taylor – look back with a certain amount of embarrassment. One of the most unforgettable numbers – for all the wrong reasons – was 'We Are Most Important Cavemen', which saw the subsequent cream of British comedy cavorting around the stage in fur loin-cloths.

Chapman and Cleese produced a dozen or so highly regarded skits during their university days, including the 'Mountaineering Sketch', and secured the pairing a decent reputation with the Footlighters – a satisfying U-turn for the two 'rejects'. (Chapman, himself rejected after a Footlights audition, wrote and performed his legendary one-man wrestling sketch at a Smoker's Concert and was invited to join the group.)

The success of *Double Take* indirectly led to the following year's Footlight revue, *Cambridge Circus*, which recruited Cleese as writer and

performer. The show took the West End by storm and toured in the USA and New Zealand. Perhaps most importantly, it was broadcast on BBC Radio. Cleese remembers: 'I very nearly didn't do the show ... especially because I hadn't done much work that year. I thought I might fail the exams. But in the end I did the show and, to my surprise, after I got off stage and went up to the Footlights club room to have a drink, there were two very nice men in dark suits. They said, "How would you like to come and work for the BBC as a writer and a producer?" It was most interesting because they'd noticed I'd written the material and it was that, rather than the performance side, that had attracted them. I said, "Well, why not!" I thought I could sell the idea to my parents because it was the BBC and there was a pension plan! It was like joining the Civil Service, and, besides, from a money point of view they were offering me £30 a week. If I'd gone into the law, I'd have got £12 a week.'

Those 'two very nice men in dark suits' were producers Peter Titheradge and Ted Taylor, and Cleese's first assignment was a Christmas radio variety special, starring Brian Rix and Terry Scott. Called *Yule Be Surprised*, it was written by Eddie McGuire, and Cleese's first task was to edit out some jokes. Soon he was being invited to add jokes to the scripts for *Emery at Large*, penning a series of monotonal bus-stop discussions between Dick Emery and Deryck Guyler. A mere four months after leaving

LEFT: Basil panics as he realises how inaccurately he has interpreted the doctors' harmless questions about holidays, in 'The Psychiatrist'.

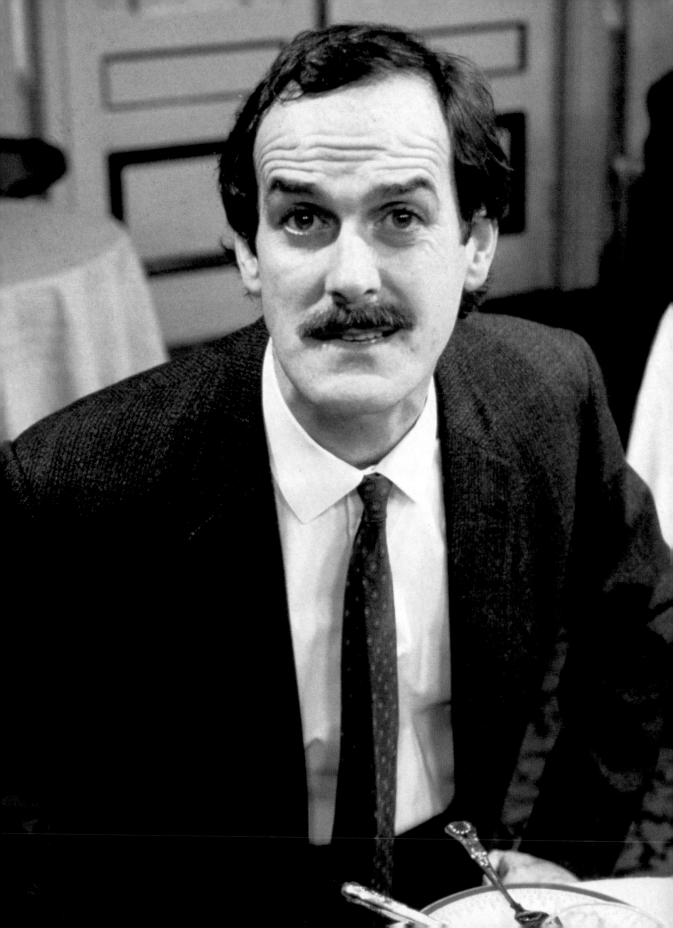

Cambridge, and despite chafing against the BBC dress code of collar and tie, Cleese was happily writing material for the Ronnie Barker and Cyril Fletcher series *Not To Worry*.

Becoming a successful comedy writer in the bosom of the BBC had its advantages, but a chance to take *Cambridge Circus* abroad in 1964 was irresistible. Following successful radio pilots for the BBC, a reshaping of the team for *I'm Sorry I'll Read That Again* and involvement in David Frost's satirical landmark *That Was the Week That Was*, Cleese went with the *Cambridge Circus* team to tour New Zealand and performed the show off-Broadway in New York. Graham Chapman and recent Cambridge graduate Eric Idle were also among the cast. Although it received positive reviews, the US run was short and most of the cast returned home. Cleese stayed on to advise the all-American replacement cast for *Cambridge Circus*, and was signed up to play the supporting role of Young Walsingham, an English upper-class twit opposite Tommy Steele in *Half a Sixpence*. Having impressed director Gene Sachs with his comic delivery, the fact that Cleese was the self-confessed worst singer in Europe didn't ruin his chances. He delivered his 30 or so lines with style, and his singing was restricted to the chorus. When even that proved too much for the rest of the cast to bear, Sachs allowed Cleese to simply mouth the lyrics. The show opened at the O'Keefe Center, Toronto, in February 1965.

The rest of his American sabbatical included a brief stint writing obituaries for the International Affairs Department of *Newsweek* magazine and a spell with John Morris's touring production of *The American Establishment Review* which recycled old Peter Cook material for the US market. While preparing to return home, Cleese was contacted by David Frost, who was putting together a comedy revue series to showcase Ronnie Barker and Ronnie Corbett. *The Frost Report*, as it was to be called, was in its embryonic stages, and Cleese was invited on board as a scriptwriter and performer. The rest is, of course, history.

The show's upper-class, middle-class and lower-class sketch, featuring Cleese, Barker and an 'I know my place' Corbett, has passed into the comedy classic archive, and Cleese's portrayal of pompous politicians, dim television interviewers and the like made him something of a small-screen star. In 1967, the *Sunday Telegraph* pinpointed Cleese's non-comedic appearance when it described him as being 'like an accountant who in his spare time is a bit fierce on the tennis court'. Frost was keen to capitalize on the success of Cleese, and began formulating a sketch show for him. Nervous at the prospect of carrying a show on his own, Cleese decided to join forces with old Cambridge pals, Tim Brooke-Taylor and Graham Chapman, and to recruit the distinctive comic genius of Marty Feldman, co-writer of *Round the Horne*. The quartet that would star in two series of ITV's *At Last the 1948 Show* was complete. They produced some classic material, and a number of sketches (including 'Bookshop' and 'The Four Yorkshiremen') were later resurrected for *Monty Python* live shows across the world. Cleese's portrayals in these groundbreaking

sketches ranged from a manic schoolmaster in 'Top of the Form' to a dragged-up constable in 'Undercover Policeman'. His sarcastic television quizmaster, Nosmo Claphanger, terrorized the aged couple of Marty Feldman and Tim Brooke-Taylor with a biting cry of 'We cares what you think!' and Cleese's notoriously bad singing was cringe makingly displayed in the self-penned classics 'The Ferret Song' and 'The Rhubarb Tart Song'.

At Last the 1948 Show was a huge success and created useful TV opportunities for its stars. Feldman was subsequently headhunted by the BBC for his own sketch series, *It's Marty*. Cleese was enlisted on the writing team, and also contributed material to the Graeme Garden series *Twice a Fortnight* and *Broaden Your Mind* which, in effect, led its three principals,

Garden, Tim Brooke-Taylor and Bill Oddie, to form the Goodies. He was also working on the radio smash *I'm Sorry I'll Read That Again*, but the studio audience's readiness to groan with pleasure at the most awful puns eventually drove him to distraction. Indeed, the Bill Oddie/Graeme Garden-scripted rants for Cleese merely reflected how he felt about the deliciously corny material. But after a three-year break, Cleese returned to the fold for one final series, and even guest-starred opposite his old Cambridge pals in the legendary 1973 Christmas special *The Goodies and the Beanstalk*. He made a climactic surprise appearance as the turbaned Genie of the Lamp, and with his tongue in his cheek, he condemned the Goodies as peddling a 'kid's programme'. Fifteen years later Cleese rejoined the team for a one-off reunion to mark the 25th anniversary of *I'm Sorry I'll Read That Again*.

Cleese's association with his Cambridge co-stars continued through the late 1960s. He, along with Chapman, Brooke-Taylor and Oxford recruit Michael Palin, was cast in David Frost's *How to Irritate People*, a special produced for US television and utilizing *1948 Show* material. With Dr Graham Chapman he also co-wrote the first ever episode of Humphrey Barclay's situation comedy *Doctor in the House*, before handing over the writing to Graeme Garden, Bill Oddie and Barry Cryer.

On television, Cleese regularly appeared on other people's shows, notably with his Goon heroes as a straight-faced announcer in the televised recreation of *A Tale of Men's Shirts*. He also found time to play one of Robin Hood's merry men opposite Peter Cook and Dudley Moore in *Goodbye Again*, guest-starred as the egg-obsessed Marcus Pugman in *The Avengers*, and appeared in several films: *Interlude*, *The Best House in London* and *The Statue*. He and Chapman had also written material for and appeared in the Peter Sellers and Ringo Starr celebration of excess, *The Magic Christian*. They went on to script and feature in the Peter Cook satire on David Frost's media clout, *The Rise and Rise of Michael Rimmer*.

On 5 October 1969, BBC Television unleashed a comic collective that would conquer the world and remain with Cleese

OPPOSITE: *Fawlty Towers* in production filming 'Gourmet Night' in north-west London.

RIGHT: 'Well … may I ask you what you were hoping to see out of a Torquay hotel bedroom window?' Basil and Mrs Richards lock horns once again.

forevermore. *Monty Python's Flying Circus* recruited Cleese, Chapman, Idle, Palin and Jones, plus the American animator Terry Gilliam, for an untried and untested series of 13 half-hours. Nobody, not even the Pythons themselves, had a firm idea of what the show was going to be about, and that was the whole point. That first series saw Cleese interview distinguished film director Sir Edward Ross (played with gruff disbelief by Graham Chapman), bring life to a moronic chef who apologizes about a dirty fork, and, most famously of all, tackle Michael Palin's shifty pet shop owner about a recently purchased Norwegian Blue parrot who seems to be rather 'bereft of life'.

ABOVE: Sybil and Polly discuss the merits of therapy while Basil looks on in bemusement in 'The Psychiatrist'.

RIGHT: Basil's lonely vigil in 'The Wedding Party'.

OPPOSITE: John Cleese as Sherlock Holmes in 'Elementary, My Dear Watson'.

The first series, although hardly a mainstream smash, proved popular enough to warrant another two batches of 13 half-hours, and allowed Cleese to silly-walk into comedy immortality, rant on about every cheese known to man, and flop for England as the lupin-mad highwayman Dennis Moore. In fact *Monty Python* established all its stars as British comedy icons. If Cleese had done nothing else in the 30 years since the series, he would still be remembered for his contribution to a show that was truly something completely different. He remembers his *Python* years with wary pride: 'I loved the first series of *Python*. It was one of the most exciting times of my life because it was as though someone had opened the gate to a field of flowers that no one had picked before, and you were able to sort of gambol through the gate and there were flowers everywhere. We had entered a new territory and it was as though almost everything we thought of felt original.

'But then, after a year, I felt that we were repeating ourselves. By the second series I was making noises to that effect. I could identify a lot of the sketches, and that defeated the whole purpose of *Python*. I'd say, "That sketch is that one from the first series plus that one from the first series, plus a little bit of that from the second series." I felt we were just combining the material we'd already done. However, the others were happy and they didn't really listen to me. I wasn't keen on doing a third series, but I agreed to be in the first six or seven, and then, because of pressure from the others, I agreed to the whole series of 13. But I felt that I wrote only two genuinely original sketches with

Graham Chapman in that series – one was "The Cheese Shop" and the other was "Dennis Moore". Everything else was a mixture of previous material, and I got very bored when that happened. I eventually said I didn't want to do any more television, and two of the guys were very cross with me. That was because they were insecure about their future outside the group.'

During the fledgling *Python* years, Cleese undertook a variety of other work. He agreed to guest-star in a single episode of the BBC comedy *Misleading Cases* in order to work alongside one of his acting heroes, Alastair Sim,

and played a humorous Sherlock Holmes opposite Willie Rushton in Barry Took's *Comedy Playhouse* episode 'Elementary, My Dear Watson'. The successful episode from this series was the *Last of the Summer Wine* pilot, and some 25 years later, with the show still running, Cleese featured in a blink-and-you'll-miss-him guest spot in the 1993 Christmas Special. His writing commissions included a one-off episode of the Ronnie Barker vehicle *Six Dates with Barker* and several episodes of the situation comedy *Doctor at Large*. It was at this time too that he established a training film company, Video Arts, which was to prove highly successful. Cleese had dropped out of the *Python* team before their six-part 1974 series and, instead, found himself stooging for Les Dawson. He returned to the group for the cheerful historical romp *Monty Python and the Holy Grail*. French taunters, the Black Knight, Tim the Wizard and Sir Lancelot were just some of the characters blessed with the Cleese touch.

The following year, BBC2 proudly presented Cleese's first and only regular situation comedy, a short television series dealing with an irascible hotelier in Torquay, called *Fawlty Towers*. Despite the gruelling writing and performing schedule for the series, Cleese still found time for other work. In 1976 he founded the Amnesty International benefit concerts, starting with *A Poke in the Eye with a Sharp Stick*, for which he recruited many old friends and revived a lot of vintage material. As the second series of *Fawlty Towers* was coming to fruition, Cleese made a brief appearance in the *Doctor Who* adventure, *City of Death* —

another landmark to add to the CV already groaning with high spots: he had mucked about with *The Muppets*, walked on by in *Ripping Yarns*, played six parts in *Whoops Apocalypse* and briefly appeared as Basil Fawlty in the pilot of *Not the Nine O'Clock News*.

Back with the *Monty Python* team, Cleese had taken time out to write (in the Bahamas) and film (in Tunisia) *Monty Python's Life of Brian*. This audacious and irreverent look at life in biblical times ('What have the Romans ever done for us?') offended most religious denominations, but is still widely regarded as one of the funniest films ever made.

The supporting film, a hilarious mock travelogue called *Away From It All*, written and narrated by Cleese under the pseudonym Nigel Farquar-Bennett, is a little-known, but proud achievement for Cleese. Building gradually from cheesy globe-trotting commentary beginnings to an intense, manic climax, it is an intriguing and brilliantly sustained piece of work.

In the early 1980s Cleese found himself increasingly called upon to enliven other people's films with an eccentric cameo or off-the-wall supporting turn. Following *The Great Muppet Caper* in 1981, he was recruited to the fantasy classic *Time Bandits*, written by Terry Gilliam and Michael Palin. Cleese was perfectly cast as a frightfully cheerful and considerate Robin Hood, who milks his Goody-Two-Shoes image for all it's worth. In 1983 Cleese was cast in a film of Peter Nichols' celebrated play concerning wartime entertainment in the services, *Privates on Parade*. Full of steely-eyed determination, incomprehension of the limp-wristed behaviour around him and awfully

apologetic comments to all and sundry, he was the embodiment of an upper-class British officer. Reluctantly persuaded to deliver a semi-silly walk for the out-take-styled closing credits, many trailers, particularly the US one, seized on the footage to advertise the film as a *Python* comedy. Although the production company didn't object, Cleese was appalled.

Wounded by controversy but wealthy after *Life of Brian*, the Python team re-formed to present their most ambitious and most disjointed film venture of all – *Monty Python's The Meaning of Life*. Cleese highlights included a sinister Death, an earnest schoolmaster giving a very practical sex education lesson, and the coolly efficient waiter who feeds Terry Jones's Mr Creosote to explosion point.

In 1985 Cleese published a collection of his best-loved sketches, *The Golden Skits of Wing Commander Muriel Volestrangler FRHS and Bar*,

while co-writing, with his therapist Robin Skynner, two self-help books called *Families and How to Survive Them* and *Life and How to Survive It*. In the USA, Cleese flirted with British cowboy eccentricity in *Silverado* alongside Kevin Costner and Kevin Kline, guest-starred in *Cheers* and cropped up as a fantasy bartender in the underrated comedy *The Big Picture*. Back in England, he starred in the cod *Fawlty Towers* film *Clockwise*, which was well received, but overshadowed by his most personal movie to date. *A Fish Called Wanda*, co-written and directed by the legendary Ealing director Charles Crichton, teamed him with Michael Palin, Jamie Lee Curtis and Kevin Kline. Its mixture of farce, heist, pomposity and fish food proved irresistible and became an international hit. Other film appearances followed, including two for director Terry Jones – *Erik the Viking*, with Cleese as the loveable villain Halfden the Black, and *The Wind in the Willows* with a Cleese cameo as a barrister. These were complemented by *Bullseye* for Michael Winner, *Yellowbeard* for Mel Damski and *Mary Shelley's Frankenstein* for Kenneth Branagh. It wasn't until 1997 that Cleese again wrote and starred in his own vehicle, *Fierce Creatures* – an 'equal not a sequel' to *A Fish Called Wanda* with the same trio of co-stars. Cleese also found himself a popular choice for cartoon voice-over work, playing a smooth-talking snake for *In the Beginning*, a villainous cat by the name of Cat R Waul in *An American Tail: Fievel Goes West*, and the French frog Jean-Bob in *The Swan Princess*.

Recent television work has included a reprise of the dead parrot sketch with Michael Palin for *Saturday Night Live*, a 30th reunion *Python Night* for BBC2, a couple of guest appearances in *3rd Rock from the Sun*, and a major BBC series *The Human Face*, which teamed him with colleagues from the past, Michael Palin and Prunella Scales. On film he played R, the bumbling sidekick to Desmond Llewellyn in the 19th James Bond adventure, *The World is not Enough,* and featured in the all-star American chase comedy *Rat Race.*

Fawlty Towers co-star Andrew Sachs remembers Cleese as 'a generous-spirited man. He's very good with other actors, welcoming even the bit-part players, making them part of the team. I know he was having some difficulties because he was separating from his wife, Connie Booth, during the making of the show, but you would never have known. He did, understandably, get quite uptight because a lot was riding on the show. By the time the audience was wheeled in, we'd have done a full day's work: does this gag work? Do we have to make last-minute changes? If he mistimed a gag, it could be painful with the frying-pan, for example, because he'd hit me instead of stopping short. I watched some of *Fawlty Towers* recently and I can see now that John was immensely strong. The way he manhandled me, lifting me up, throwing me down, was brilliant.'

Surprisingly, John Cleese has often reflected that, unlike most of his fellow Oxbridge generation, his work output has been rather limited. But for someone who has been involved, through both acting and writing, with the film voted funniest of the millennium (*Monty Python's Life of Brian*) and the television series voted the best of all time (*Fawlty Towers*), this hardly seems to matter.

PRUNELLA SCALES
SYBIL FAWLTY

'My little nest of vipers'
Basil to Sybil

ADISTINGUISHED and versatile actress, Prunella Scales has been somewhat cursed by journalistic shorthand, which insists on comparing or contrasting every new role with her most infamous and celebrated creation, Sybil Fawlty. For a performer who has worked consistently for some 50 years and spanned the gamut from situation comedy to Shakespeare, to be best known for a mere 12 half-hours of television can be frustrating. Scales, however, takes it all in her professional stride. Her husband, the actor Timothy West, is amazed when asked if his wife is really like Sybil Fawlty. His usual reaction is a sigh, a shrug of the shoulders and a wry, 'I should hope not.'

Still, whatever her drawbacks, Sybil is a performance to be proud of. Scales maintains a fine balance in her portrayal, allowing us to see both the monster in woman's clothing that Basil believes he has married, and the sociable, capable hotelier her guests encounter. Basil might characterize Sybil as the only woman in the world who can make toast simply by breathing on it, but we can very much sympathize with the relatively normal lower-middle-class girl who married Basil and has been making the best of it ever since. We are glad Sybil is thick-skinned enough to survive the continual snide comments muttered by her long-suffering husband. Cleese believes that the relationship could stand the insults: '"My little nest of vipers" – I always liked that one. It was funny because you never really minded the things that Basil said to Sybil because she was never hurt by them. If she had been, then it wouldn't have worked. There's a certain degree of discomfort that people can tolerate in

comedy, but they don't want to see anyone in real pain. It was water off a duck's back. She just didn't give a damn, so although the insults were funny, they were fundamentally ineffectual. That's why we could get away with them.'

Though some of her mannerisms are genuinely irritating, her calm and dismissive responses to Basil's neuroses are heartening proof that sanity does ultimately reign at *Fawlty Towers*, even if it does occasionally take time off for ingrowing toenails.

Scales' own contribution to the character was paramount. John Cleese recalls that the

ABOVE: Prunella Scales and John Cleese reunited for *The Human Face*, which was broadcast in 2001.

RIGHT: Joan Sanderson, Prunella Scales and Gerry Cowper promote the radio series of *After Henry*.

Sybil he wrote was very different from the finished article: 'Connie and I had a different conception of the character from the way Pru played it at the first read-through. I remember going home and saying to Connie, "What do you think about the way Pru's playing it?" and her saying, "Well, it's not what we thought of." Actually, we were both a bit worried, and then after about two days we actually saw that what Pru was doing worked better than the way we thought it would be played. So that helped us because when we came to write the second episode and the rest of the series, we began to have her voice in our ear. We didn't have Pru's rendition when we wrote the first one.'

She was also responsible for Sybil's braying laugh. Cleese recalls: 'Pru began to develop a laugh, and I think she and I talked about it a bit at one point. I remember it was a deep "ah, ah, ah, huh, huh" and I described it in the script for "The Wedding Party" as somebody machine-gunning a seal, which I thought was a very good description of it. Again, that was something we worked on and that was the delight of going into shows after we'd done one or two. We were able to borrow from what the actors and actresses were beginning to create.'

Prunella Scales was born Prunella Margaret Rumney Illingworth on 22 June 1932, in Sutton Abingers, Surrey. The daughter of actress Catherine Scales, performing was clearly in the blood, and theatrical talent became evident during her education at Moira House, Eastbourne. After training at the Old Vic Theatre School and the exclusive Herbert Berghof Studio in New York, her first taste of stage work came with rep assignments in Huddersfield, Salisbury, Oxford and Bristol.

Prunella started film work early with a featured role in the 1952 sub-Ealing comedy tale *Laxdale Hall*. Starring the redoubtable Raymond Huntley, the film was reminiscent of *Whiskey Galore!* in its story of Hebridean islanders with an aversion to paying road tax. Prunella's most interesting early film appearance came in the 1954 David Lean production of *Hobson's Choice* where she excelled as one of bombastic Charles Laughton's daughters. Other small parts followed, including roles in the Laurence Harvey and Simone Signoret melodrama *Room at the Top* (1959) and the relaxed Peter Sellers costume comedy *The Waltz of the Toreadors* (1962).

It was television, however, that would make her name, starting with a regular role in *Coronation Street* as Ellen Hughes. She went on to work with many comedy greats, including Jimmy Edwards, Ronnie Barker, June Whitfield, Dick Emery and Paul Eddington.

Marrying Timothy West at the Chelsea Register Office in 1963 (with, spookily, Scales wearing a hat borrowed from the wife of Andrew Sachs), the year also saw Prunella's first major success in television comedy. She was teamed with Richard Briers for a specially created situation comedy called *Marriage Lines*. The pair played Kate and George Starling, newlyweds struggling with rather predictable domestic problems, but the writing and endearing performances lent the series a winning charm. During the fifth, and what turned out to be the final series, Prunella was pregnant, so the happy event was written into the episodes. Typically, the shows had proved

popular enough to warrant a transfer to radio so Briers and Scales made two series of 13 episodes before the sitcom was finally pensioned off in 1967.

Seasons at Stratford-upon-Avon, and work, as both actress and director, on the London stage and at the Chichester Festival heightened her growing reputation as a consummate stage professional, with credits including *The Promise* and Noel Coward's *Hay Fever*.

Back in television comedy, 1973 saw Prunella playing Marion Joyce, the dictatorial wife of Ronnie Barker in *Seven of One*. This was followed by a *Comedy Playhouse* episode 'The Big Job', starring Peter Jones as an incompetent petty criminal and Scales as his deftly thieving wife. Under the experienced comedy eye of producer Dennis Main Wilson the pilot was made into a series, *Mr Big*, and aired from January 1977. A second series appeared from June 1977 but the format failed to catch on. Although short-lived, it nonetheless acted as a bridge for Scales between two series of *Fawlty Towers*.

Stage credits during the decade included *It's a Two Foot Six Inches Above the Ground World*, the film version of which, *The Love Ban*, featured John Cleese. Other stage work included *The Wolf* in 1975 and *Breezeblock Park* in 1978, while Prunella continued to make her mark as an accomplished character actress in

ABOVE: Prunella Scales and Richard Briers in *Marriage Lines*.

LEFT: Husband and wife Timothy West and Prunella Scales in Joe Orton's *What the Butler Saw*

OPPOSITE: Prunella Scales with Peter Jones in *Mr Big*.

British film. She appeared in the 1976 Walt Disney pony-rescue weepie *Escape from the Dark*, starring Alastair Sim in his final screen role. The following year she was cast in the outrageously camp Peter Cook and Dudley Moore re-telling of *The Hound of the Baskervilles*, which had one of the most outstanding comedy casts ever assembled (Terry-Thomas, Kenneth Williams, Spike Milligan, Max Wall, Roy Kinnear, to name but a few). Prunella cropped up opposite a flamboyantly Welsh Dr Watson from Dudley Moore, as the deadly earnest telegram code-suggesting postal worker. In contrast, Prunella's next film appearance was in *The Boys from Brazil* in which Gregory Peck played an unrepentant

Nazi and Laurence Olivier his captor.

Following the film, in 1978, Prunella appeared in *Pickersgill People*, a five-part comedy soap opera. Packed with stereotypically slow-thinking Northerners and bizarre, off-the-wall situations, it had an excellent supporting cast including Richard Wilson, Bernard Hill, Bryan Pringle and Sam Kelly.

Perhaps her most satisfying and impressive performance was on stage in 1980 when she played the title role in *An Evening with Queen Victoria*. It was a piece she would perform on and off for many years, and it was eventually recorded for a special television broadcast. Stage roles continued to allow the actress to step beyond the confines of Sybil Fawlty and flex her theatrical muscles, not least in *The Merchant of Venice* and *The Merry Wives of Windsor*. Many other stage and television roles followed, but she was particularly acclaimed in a 1985 small-screen adaptation of Alan Ayckbourn's *Absurd Person Singular* as the incoherent dipsomaniac Marion Brewster-Wright. She then re-established herself as a TV favourite in two series of the classic comedy drama *Mapp and Lucia* with Geraldine McEwan and Nigel Hawthorne. Based on the stories of E.F. Benson, the series had old-style charm, sophistication and wit.

It was in 1988 that Prunella landed her longest-running situation-comedy role, as Sarah France in 38 episodes of the hit ITV show *After Henry*. The series had started as a radio programme, and Prunella commented at the time that 'these are scripts of rare economy and distinction.' Written by Simon Brett, the series chronicled the tragi-comic happenings in

the life of a 42-year-old widow (Scales) living with her mother (Joan Sanderson) and daughter (Gerry Cowper) and working in a book shop owned by the charming Russell (Benjamin Whitrow). By the time the series ended in March 1989 the show had already

OPPOSITE: Basil and Sybil bicker over the hotel's 'no riff-raff' policy in 'Gourmet Night'.

ABOVE: 'No, no, it's lovely, it's just a bit buttery with my skin.' Sybil attends to the finer points of hotel management.

transferred to television with Jonathan Newth replacing Whitrow and Janine Wood stepping into the shoes of Cowper. The BBC, rather surprisingly, turned down the potential television series, and it was Thames who bought the rights, producing one of the best-loved sitcoms of the decade. Scales and Sanderson created fine comedy performances from the scripts, and the series is still fondly remembered.

On film through the 1980s, Prunella chalked up a number of interesting appearances, including the Faye Dunaway remake of *The Wicked Lady* in 1982, and the moving Maggie Smith melodrama *The Lonely Passion of Judith Hearne* in 1987. Other film roles came in *My Friend Walter, Second Best, Wolf,* and *An Awfully Big Adventure*. She camped it up as the bespectacled and heavily made-up secretary of Freddie Jones's manic chocolate factory owner in *Consuming Passions*, and gave her finest film performance to date, as the sex-starved, am-dram actress in Alan Ayckbourn's *A Chorus of Disapproval* (1989) with Jeremy Irons and Anthony Hopkins.

In 1992 Prunella featured in Merchant Ivory's lavish production of *Howards End*, later displaying a talent for self-parody when she played the frightfully buttoned-up Aunt Agnes in *Stiff Upper Lips*, a Merchant Ivory spoof with her son, Sam West, and Peter Ustinov.

The 1990s were filled with memorable stage performances, not least in *School for Scandal* and *Long Day's Journey into Night*, the latter opposite Timothy West. Scales' emotive performance as Mary Cavan Tyrone won great critical acclaim.

As ever, Prunella made many television appearances too. It was in 1991 that she gave what many consider her finest television performance, as Queen Elizabeth II in Alan Bennett's take on the Anthony Blunt scandal, *A Question of Attribution*. Continuing in 'genteel' mode, she appeared as Miss Bates in the 1997 adaptation of Jane Austen's *Emma*.

Back in comedy, Prunella played the lead role of 'Mrs' Tilston in Carla Lane's ITV series *Searching*. Set in a therapy centre, it mixed belly laughs with feminism and psychology. Described by Scales as a 'drama-doc-sit-trag', the premise did not catch on and was pulled after the first series. Back on slightly safer ground, Prunella joined the cast of the political satire series *Look at the State We're In*, produced by John Cleese. She then played Caroline Aherne's mother in *The World of Lee Evans*.

The fine and enduring quality of Prunella's work was officially recognized when she was awarded a CBE in the 1992 Honours List. She is currently enjoying popularity as the elderly fusspot of the long-running Tesco commercials alongside Jane Horrocks. Prunella Scales continues to give first-class performances in a staggering variety of roles, but in the hearts and minds of a nation there is an image of her that is forever Sybil.

OPPOSITE: Queen of all she surveys … Sybil remains firmly in control.

ANDREW SACHS
MANUEL

**'Do you think I could do a German waiter,
because I can't do a Spanish accent.'**

Andrew Sachs to John Cleese

As with Prunella Scales, the distinguished acting career of Andrew Sachs has, to some extent, been overshadowed by the spectre of *Fawlty Towers*. Sachs as Manuel was an instant hit and has remained one of the most endearing and indelible images of television. Fumbling, stooping, gibbering, but ever optimistic, Manuel's cheap and cheerful hired hand exacerbates the chaos of hotel life, while also providing Basil with a scapegoat on whom to lay the blame for every disaster. Manuel acts partly to reveal the true natures of the other principal characters. Sybil responds to him with indifference, Polly with real, if exasperated kindness, and Basil by bullying this vulnerable dependant and thereby exposing his own innate cowardice.

Sachs recalls: 'The fact he came from Barcelona was developed during rehearsal, but

I remember saying to John Cleese, "Do you think I could do a German waiter, because I can't do a Spanish accent." He actually considered it – or pretended to.' The actor behind the Spaniard was actually born in Berlin on 7 April 1930. With a German-Jewish father and a Christian, half-Austrian mother, his native country was not the ideal place to be growing up during the 1930s, so the family moved to England. Sachs returned to Germany in 1958, the year he met his future wife, dance-school teacher Melody, because 'I felt interested and curious, but realized I was a foreigner. I've a great love for this country. I don't think I'd have been happy as a German actor. It's terribly serious. I'd rather be an actor in English.' His burning ambition to get into the business from an early age divided his parents: 'My father would have insisted I got proper qualifications,

The Fawlty school of staff training.

and whisk me off to Beverly Hills', Sachs first found success in comedy with featured roles in Brian Rix farces. Indeed, one of his earliest ventures into television was in a series called *Dial RIX* , where the cast list also included Elspet Gray, Terry Scott, Patrick Cargill, and Basil Fawlty's hard-of-hearing harridan Joan Sanderson.

Perhaps Sachs' most prestigious theatrical venture came in 1973, when he appeared opposite Alec Guinness in Alan Bennett's *Habeas Corpus*. It was in this production that John Cleese spotted Sachs' potential for *Fawlty Towers*: 'I'd seen Andrew and he just made me laugh till I hurt. I realized how good he was at physical comedy, and so I got him. He just touched the character with so much soul. Andrew is a very quiet and immensely thoughtful man. He's extraordinarily kind, very considerate and rather introverted. Then he put that moustache on and suddenly, "Ding!", this energy exploded. He was Manuel. Something just comes through that you don't normally see.'

It was the year after *Habeas Corpus* that Sachs landed the role that would make and keep him a star – the manic Spanish waiter Manuel: 'My job was to get laughs. What you learned was to get the best laugh out of an audience – and that was very exciting and stimulating.' Sachs believes that 'comedy requires a sense of detachment. It's watching the man on the banana skin, rather than being the man on the banana skin, which is tragedy.'

Sachs drew on reality for his interpretation of the role, basing the character on an actor that he knew who had been dropped from a show because of his poor command of English: 'I felt

but I persuaded my mother that I was too good for ordinary labour. I was an artist and had my wonderful talents to give. And she fell for that.'

Starting his professional career as assistant stage manager at Bexhill, and fully expecting a forward-thinking impresario to 'discover me deeply for this man. He was keen to please, keen to do the right thing, but the producer was right to drop him and the actor would get over it. That's Manuel. He bounces straight back; he's a great survivor.'

Sachs had to be something of a survivor himself to get through the rigorous filming requirements for his madcap, accident-prone character. Following the shooting of a particularly arduous sequence involving a smouldering jacket in 'The Germans', Sachs suffered chemical burns and his arm was bandaged for

weeks afterwards. 'It's still quite sore if I expose [my shoulders] to the sun.'

Cleese also recalls the physical strains that Sachs underwent as Manuel: 'He took a lot of knocks, but the truth is, if you do this kind of comedy, you have to expect it. I was forever snagging my finger on door handles and stubbing my toe on the little brass strip at the bottom of the stairs. It's like playing football. I mean, you're going to get kicked here and there, and if you're doing farce, you know you're

going to get banged. Two bad things happened to Andrew. One was in the episode where there's the fire drill, the Germans episode. There was a jacket that someone fixed in the special effects department to smoke, and I'm very sorry to say that some of the acid they used to get the jacket to smoke actually got through the other side of the jacket on to Andrew's skin and burnt him. Actually the BBC paid him some damages (£700) because it was a very bad mistake.

'The other instance was my fault. We'd been practising all week with me hitting Andrew with a saucepan. I don't know why we didn't get a rubber saucepan. Still, I was using a real one and it was a big one. I was trying to hit Andrew a sliding blow and just as I started, he straightened up and I caught him a terrible one. I'm afraid he had a headache for about two days, but Andrew's sensible enough to know that that's going to happen.'

Indeed, Sachs has nothing but good memories of his time as the manic waiter with the clumsy manner. Although it may have pigeonholed him in the eyes of the public, casting directors have seen past this single comic characterization to find the fine actor within. Sachs himself is delighted that his performance didn't spill over into real life: 'When *Fawlty Towers* was at its height, I was sitting in the tube opposite a girl who was describing the previous night's episode to her friend, frequently looking in my direction ... and she didn't recognize me. I thought that was quite nice.'

OPPOSITE: Basil attempts to get through to Manuel ... 'Well, he's hopeless, isn't he. You might as well ask the cat.'

In 1977 Sachs appeared in the seven-part Yorkshire Television sketch series *Took and Co*, a vehicle to showcase the writing and performing talent of Barry Took. When the second series of *Fawlty Towers* was agreed with Cleese and Booth, Sachs was again an integral part of the mix. With the dawn of the 1980s and the end of *Fawlty Towers*, Sachs found himself much in demand for television work. Cast in the leading role of *Dead Ernest* as ill-fated schoolteacher Ernest Springer, Sachs played a football pools winner killed by a champagne cork hitting him squarely between the eyes. The rest of the seven-part series detailed the eccentric and downright odd characters Ernest meets in the afterlife, including decomposing composers, the Archangel Derek, and John Le Mesurier in one of his last roles as the Head of Plagues. The rather bizarre premise didn't gel with the public, so a second series was never commissioned.

In October 1982 Sachs joined an all-star cast including Bernard Cribbins, Irene Handl, Richard Briers and Jimmy Edwards to support Eric Sykes and Tommy Cooper in *It's Your Move*. Produced by the man behind *The Benny Hill Show*, Dennis Kirkland, and written and directed by Eric Sykes, this proved to be a popular Thames comedy spectacular.

Life in 1980s situation comedy was a bit difficult for Sachs. Still surrounded by video releases and repeat screenings of *Fawlty Towers* his choice of work reflected his desire to avoid typecasting. He later opted to play a flustered businessman in *There Comes A Time...* who discovers he is suffering from an incurable disease – not exactly the most hilarious notion for a comedy series. Again, it was a short-lived outing.

Another ill-fated situation comedy came along in 1993 when Sachs was cast in the leading role of Nat Silver in *Every Silver Lining*. The credentials looked good. *Blackadder* director, Richard Boden, was the producer, and *Rising Damp* actress Frances de la Tour was cast as Sachs' wife. However, the premise was weak and over-written, with the stars playing a continually arguing Jewish couple desperately trying to keep their heads above the financial waters as their East End café faces the recession. Sachs was luckier with the children's fantasy *Pirates* when he was cast as the dashing Basmati Bill. The series ran for three years, and Sachs' swashbuckling showed that his comic touch was as deft as ever.

Sachs' work in films has been sporadic to say the least, although it includes some interesting credits. At the age of 15 he appeared in the 1946 Ealing comedy, *Hue and Cry*. He then cropped up as surprise, surprise, a Spanish waiter in the big-screen version of *Are You Being Served?* (1977) and followed this with the 1978 sex comedy *What's Up SuperDoc?* The latter was notable largely for its cast of comedy favourites, including Christopher Mitchell, Melvyn Hayes, Bill Pertwee and Harry H. Corbett. He later appeared in Mel Brooks' 1981 film *History of the World Part 1*, and followed this with the more prestigious black comedy *Consuming Passions,* based on the Michael Palin and Terry Jones-scripted television piece, *Secrets.*

It's hardly surprising that Sachs is best remembered for his performance as Manuel. He has recreated his role more times than any other actor associated with the series. When the BBC Audio Collection decided to release the *Fawlty Towers* soundtracks on tape, Sachs was drafted in to provide Manuel's observations and linking narration to make sense of the more visual aspects of the episodes. Sachs has also used his Manuel persona to try to dent the British pop charts. Although they made little impact, the four singles Sachs released have become collector's items among fans. The first, 'Manuel's Good Food Guide', was released in 1977. Two years later, under the name of Manuel and Los Por Favors, he released the shamefully bad 'O Cheryl'. Even worse was to come. In 1981 Sachs recorded a Manuel version of Joe Dolce's annoyingly popular 'Shaddap You Face'. Unfortunately it was hit by a court injunction and prevented from being released before Dolce's original had hit the charts. When the Manuel version finally came out it sadly managed to reach only 138 in the UK charts.

On stage, Sachs has recreated Manuel for various charitable causes, including *The Secret Policeman's Third Ball*, an Amnesty International benefit at the London Palladium in March 1987. In it he performed a specially written monologue reflecting on his beloved adopted country, and sang a shortened version of 'Ode to England', the B side of his 1979 single. The character has also been used in several commercials to promote anything from British building societies to Australian wine. The scripts for these bring back a perfect sense of Manuel's eager incompetence as, when asked for Carte D'Or, he makes a hasty exit, there are noises off-stage of ripping metal, and Sachs returns with an enthusiastic 'See, I bring you car door!'

Basil rallies the troops in an attempt to avert yet another panic in the kitchen in 'Gourmet Night'.

John Cleese believes Manuel is an eternal character: 'I recently stayed in a hotel in Jersey that was run entirely for the convenience of the staff. That's an attitude that has permeated a lot of British institutions. One of the points I was trying to make with Manuel was not that he was some kind of an idiot. What annoyed me when I went into a lot of British hotels and restaurants (particularly one chain of steak houses) was that almost nobody there spoke any English at all. So the chances of you getting what you ordered were about one in six. I knew the reason – it wasn't that the foreigners were stupid: it was that the owners were not prepared to pay proper salaries, so they got people who were desperate for any kind of

work. The owners didn't bother to train them and they didn't bother to make sure they could speak English properly. That was the fundamental joke about Basil and Manuel. Manuel is one of the sweetest people. He's always trying to get it right. There's no way you can blame him. It's just that his English is not quite as good as it might be and that's the fault of Basil, not Manuel.'

Despite firmly believing that over-repeating *Fawlty Towers* cost him the plum role of Victor Meldrew in *One Foot in the Grave*, Sachs has great affection for the character of Manuel. Indeed, in the early 1990s he and his stepson, broadcaster John Sachs, were writing a pilot for a sitcom based entirely on Manuel. John Sachs was to play the part of Manuel, while Andrew would restrict his contribution to script-writing and cameo appearances. It was even rumoured that John Cleese would act as a consultant on the project, but sadly nothing came of the plans. However, Sachs' most famous alter-ego has certainly not prevented him from winning roles of a much more serious nature. In 2000, he gave what many people consider to be one of his finest performances, as a meek and extremely troubled Holocaust survivor in *Silent Witness*. Fittingly, he then narrated the Radio 4 documentary series *The Jewish Journey,* a personal look at the history of Jewish life in Britain. It was also fitting, in light of his connection with comedy's best-loved hotel, that Sachs narrated the very first in a long line of BBC docu-soaps, *Hotel,* filmed in Liverpool's Adelphi.

On stage, Sachs has happily toured the country with his one-man show *Fawlty Years On* since September 2000. Now called *Life After Fawlty* Sachs insists: 'We have to make sure the audience don't expect two hours of Manuel.' In fact the show is a refreshing and stimulating theatrical experience which includes a monologue on the ways to survive the pain and pleasure of being a Spanish waiter, but also involves a Victorian-style recitation of Tennyson's epic poem *Enoch Arden*: 'A tear-jerker, a story of old-fashioned values,' according to Sachs. 'In between, we'll dip into other classic verse, invite you to groan at some terrible doggerel, get groovy with Gershwin, bewitched by Beethoven, and thrill to a great short story ... or two.'

Over the years Sachs has repeatedly resisted the temptation to earn big bucks from making a long-running, American networked presentation of Manuel, and continues to do so. 'Thirty-eight weeks for five years playing a Spanish waiter? Not if it was a million pounds an episode.'

Andrew Sachs and Frances de la Tour in a publicity shot for *Every Silver Lining*.

CONNIE BOOTH
POLLY

'Connie's understanding of structure in the scripts was absolutely vital.'
John Howard Davies

THE sane centre of life at *Fawlty Towers* is Polly, the low-paid and much put-upon chambermaid whom Basil relies on and Manuel looks up to. Her loyalty to, and tolerance of, Basil, in the face of Sybil's wrath, can often put her in a difficult position, as can her defence of Manuel. Polly is the middlewoman of the hotel, protecting the other principals from each other's worst excesses. Often overlooked and underrated thanks to her subtle performance and less showy dialogue, Connie Booth's contribution to the nation's favourite sitcom, as both actor and writer, is immeasurable. Her co-writer, co-star and ex-husband John Cleese believes that 'getting Connie's character right was not too difficult. She is the sensible one and she's also Basil's confidante. When he gets in terrible trouble, he will go to Polly and say this has

happened and this is what I have to achieve. It's terribly useful as a writing device to have someone to discuss the plot with, to have someone that the protagonist can go to and establish the situation with. Somebody once described Polly as the Horatio to my Hamlet.'

Connie was born in 1944 in the picturesque farming community of Indianapolis, Indiana. By the age of four, she had moved with her family to New Rochelle, New York and a decade later was fuelling her desire to became an actress by appearing in high school productions. She went on to study at the American Theater Wing in New York and appeared in Shakespeare for a San Diego drama festival. In the mid-1960s she made a few brief appearances in films, and then she met John Cleese. Many American critics considered the meeting of the young actress with the British

comedian as a curse rather than a blessing. Despite her doing some of her best-appreciated work in association with Cleese, some thought the relationship sign-posted the end of a promising dramatic career. The encounter took place when Connie was working as a waitress in a Second Avenue café, and Cleese was appearing in the Broadway production of *Half a Sixpence*. The couple married on 20 February 1968 and almost immediately began the first of many comedy collaborations together. When David Frost was showcasing British comedy talent such as Frankie Howerd, Tommy Cooper and Ronnie Barker for the American market, Cleese and Booth wrote and appeared in the one-off sketch show *How To Irritate People*, with Michael Palin Graham Chapman, Dick Vosburgh and Tim Brooke-Taylor.

Connie, naturally teamed up with her husband, played a foreshadowing of her no-nonsense *Fawlty Towers* character, as a girl gradually brought to boiling point by her boyfriend's sickening attempts to make sure she is happy.

When Cleese co-created *Monty Python* in 1969, Connie guested in four episodes. She played the besotted girl madly in love with Michael Palin's filthy Ken Shabby, the ringletted young thing brutally knocked out in the boxing ring by Cleese's manic fighter and, most memorably of all, Palin's cheerful but ultimately distraught girlfriend during 'The Lumberjack Song'. She re-created her role for the 1971 Python film *And Now for Something Completely Different*. That year also saw the birth

of a daughter, Cynthia, to her and Cleese. (Some 17 years later she appeared opposite her father in *A Fish Called Wanda* and, a decade on, in *Fierce Creatures*.)

Connie's association with *Python* continued when she appeared as the obnoxious Princess with Wooden Teeth in *Monty Python's Fliegender Zirkus or Schnappes with Everything* in October 1973. Terry Jones played her father, Graham Chapman her mother, Cleese her ill-fated suitor, and Michael Palin the buck-toothed Prince Walter, who finally claims her hand by popping down the shops to buy the king 20 Bensons. In 1974, Cleese and Booth joined forces again for the enchanting short film, *Romance with a Double Bass*. Connie played the dewy-eyed Princess Constanza, and also had a hand in the script. Connie later played the unfortunate witch in *Monty Python and the Holy Grail* – ducked and drowned if innocent, burnt at the stake if guilty. Her philosophical, 'Well, it's a fair cop,' as the mad reasoning proves her guilt is a memorable moment.

Back on the small screen, Connie played Jill in the 1976 series *The Glittering Prizes* and the following year appeared with Cleese once more in the Sherlock Holmes-inspired comedy adventure *The Strange Case of the End of Civilisation as We Know It*. She enjoyed a dual role as the femme fatale Francine Moriarty and the kindly Mrs Hudson. Also in 1977, Connie joined Cleese on stage for the Amnesty International benefit concert *An Evening Without*

LEFT: Connie Booth in the BBC costume drama *The Buccaneers*.

Sir Bernard Miles for the definitive rendition of 'The Bookshop Sketch' from *At Last The 1948 Show*. The material was subsequently released on record as *The Mermaid Frolics*.

Following the success of *Fawlty Towers* Connie was offered various roles. In 1980 she played Mrs Errol in *Little Lord Fauntleroy* and excelled as Sylvia Bassington-French in the star-studded Agatha Christie adaptation *Why Didn't They Ask Evans?* She was involved in more contemporary crime when she featured in *Bergerac*. Other television work included *The Hound of the Baskervilles*, opposite Ian Richardson's flamboyant Sherlock Holmes, *Lenny Henry Tonite* and the high profile 1995 costume drama *The Buccaneers*.

Connie's appearances on the big screen have been less prolific, but she has worked on some prestigious films. She was the Lady from Delaware in the Anthony Hopkins and Anne Bancroft long-distance romance *84 Charing Cross Road*, she appeared in Neil Jordan's haunted castle romp *High Spirits* with Peter O'Toole, teamed up with post-Bond Timothy Dalton in *Hawks*, a disturbing comedy about mental health, and was cast in Michael Palin's lyrical romance, *American Friends*.

ABOVE: Working at *Fawlty Towers* begins to take its toll on the long-suffering Polly.

BRIAN HALL
TERRY

'Look, Mr Fawlty, take it easy.'
Terry to Basil

HARD as it may be to believe, the cheerful cockney chef appeared only in the 1979 series of *Fawlty Towers*. Nonetheless, Brian Hall's short-cropped hair, ferret-like features and energetic delivery left an indelible mark on the series. His impassioned run-ins with Manuel when his supremacy of the kitchen is threatened, his muttered insults to Basil, his hidden grasp of intellectual references, his mystery-shrouded hobby, 'karate' ... He clearly had a full life outside of the only place we saw him, and that was due as much to his acting ability as to the subtlety of the scripts. Hall's contribution undoubtedly helped to fuse the four principals from the first series.

Brian Hall himself was an actor far removed from the cheerful world of television situation comedy. Like Harry H. Corbett, before small-screen fame altered his career path forever, Hall

had a track record in serious drama. A pioneer of the Royal Court, he co-wrote the emotive play *Made It Ma*. His most impressive role was in the hard-hitting gangland thriller *The Long Good Friday*. He also appeared in such TV favourites as *Softly, Softly* and *Emmerdale Farm*.

Although *Fawlty Towers* fated him to be typecast as a cheerful cockney chappie ever after, Hall never complained. He played Brian the barman in the Jim Davidson comedy *Up the Elephant and Round the Castle*, and followed that with the role of a cheerful and opportunistic milkman in the Tim Brooke-Taylor BBC vehicle *You Must Be the Husband*. Written by Colin Bostock-Smith, the two series featured Diane Keen as Tim's loving wife who finds new fame, fortune and notoriety as the author of an ultra-successful raunchy novel. Hall was perfectly cast as the milkman who continually plants seeds of doubt in Tim's mind, drops lusty remarks about the attractiveness of Tim's wife and generally raises the comic ante on each brief appearance.

Delighted at the continued success of *Fawlty Towers*, Hall, rather tongue-in-cheekily, considered his trickle of residuals less than satisfactory. He therefore penned a friendly note to John Cleese expressing his pleasure at the continual exposure but complaining that he should have earned a Rolls-Royce from the profits of the series. Cleese, tickled by the note, sent Hall a toy Rolls-Royce by return of post. Sadly, Brian Hall was diagnosed with cancer and died of the disease on 16 September 1997. He was just 59 years old.

Terry prepares breakfast with Sybil while Basil checks the use-by date on the ominous bag of kippers.

BALLARD BERKELEY
MAJOR GOWEN

'We loved this guy who was in his own world. He never quite understood what was going on, but always added his own insane interpretation of it.'

John Cleese

ONE of television's best-loved old bumblers, the Major is *Fawlty Towers'* aged patriot, who lives quite contentedly in a harmless fantasy world of his own. His preoccupations are reassuringly constant: all he ever needs to know is whether the papers have arrived or if the bar is open, and on one memorable occasion, where the dreaded Germans are. The Major's old-world, chest-puffing Britishness seems to represent a grander, yet more naive age. That age may have passed and with it the Major's credibility and position, but Berkeley's performance gives real dignity to this minor but important character.

Born in 1904, Berkeley began his film career with *The Chinese Bungalow* in 1930, a murderous melodrama starring Matheson Lang and Anna Neagle. He continued to crop up at infrequent intervals throughout the decade

with credits including *London Melody*, again with Neagle, and *The Outsider* with suave George Sanders. Quickly gaining a reputation for portraying stolid authority figures, Berkeley appeared with many illustrious names, including Athene Seyler, Bernard Miles, Margaret Lockwood and Derek Farr. In 1942 Berkeley played an engineer commander in Noel Coward's salute to the navy's war effort, *In Which We Serve*, and in 1947 was cast in Alberto Cavalcanti's grim, post-war thriller *They Made Me A Fugitive* alongside Trevor Howard. Three years later Berkeley was working with the master, Alfred Hitchcock, on *Stage Fright*, with Marlene Dietrich, Michael Wilding and Alastair Sim. The rest of the decade threw up several enjoyable quota quickies, including the 1951 chorus girl-killer mystery *The Long Dark Hall*, starring Rex

Harrison and Lili Palmer, and the 1955 Ronald Shiner vicarage farce *See How They Run*.

Berkeley's film appearances continued right through the 1950s and '60s, and he played more policemen, judges and bank managers in television drama and comedy. In 1970 he was cast as Colonel Satchwell-Simpson in the one-off *Comedy Playhouse* episode 'Haven of Rest', an Alan Melville script about an old people's home which included many great names from British theatre including Deryck Guyler, John Le Mesurier, Patricia Hayes and Joyce Carey. Although pushing 80 when *Fawlty Towers* came to an end, Berkeley was eager to keep working. He appeared as 'Uncle' Greville Hart in the second series of *To the Manor Born*, and was a semi-regular for four years in *Fresh Fields* with Julia McKenzie. His last film performance was typical – a wonderfully dithering role in *National Lampoon's European Vacation*, with fellow Brits Maureen Lipman, Robbie Coltrane, Mel Smith and Eric Idle.

Still, it was *Fawlty Towers* that endeared this crusty old professional to audiences around the world, and his portrayal of bluster and bewilderment was never better than in 'The Germans', a people whom the Major dismisses as 'bad eggs'. Part of a generation who fought for their country, he may be a 'drunken old sod' but he is a survivor of a time when Britain had an empire. Displaying the qualities that made Britain great, he emerges from his whiskey-fuddled haze and once more rallies to the cause. Little wonder that the Major is the favourite character of its creators. John Cleese recalls: 'We loved this guy who was in his own world. He never quite understood what was going on, but always added his own insane interpretation of it. I was hugely fond of Ballard Berkeley. He was a wonderful fellow, and having had a very distinguished career, it was lovely that right towards the end of it he had this huge hit. He was like me. He was an insane cricket fan. When I was in the rehearsal room with Prunella Scales, I'd glance over her shoulder and suddenly see Ballard holding up all the digits on one hand and one finger on the other. That would mean there were six Australian wickets down. I just loved that man.' He died in 1988 at the age of 84.

RENEE ROBERTS & GILLY FLOWER
MISS GATSBY & MISS TIBBS

'The old ladies were absolutely terrific.'
John Cleese

APART from the Major, the only other long-term residents at *Fawlty Towers* were the charmingly tittering old maids Miss Gatsby and Miss Tibbs – characters who appear in every episode of the series. John Cleese remembers them with great affection: 'The old ladies were absolutely terrific. It was a very happy group because everybody was very pleased with what they had to do. Nobody was trying to build their part up. Everyone was happy.'

Interestingly, the two old dears who appeared in the opening show are not only uncredited and completely without dialogue, but clearly played by different actresses from the rest of the series. Renée Roberts and Gilly Flower, who made their first appearance in the second episode of series one and stayed until the conclusion, were pros of the old school, with literally hundreds of stage and television credits to their name.

Their characters in *Fawlty Towers* have little to do save bring out Basil's condescending charm and this they do admirably. Basil's liked and respected position in the quiet lives of the two old women is one of the few things that indicate his basic humanity. He may be patronizing: during 'The Builders' episode, he explains that they have to go to another hotel for their 'din dins', and on another occasion shamelessly threatens to serve them bread and cheese while the quality stuff is reserved for the gourmet evening guests, but despite the abuse, the old ladies twitter around him, clearly delighted to be noticed and tolerating his worst excesses. Would anyone but Miss Tibbs have remained in residence after being locked in a cupboard with a corpse?

Good manners and a war-inspired sense of duty help both old dears through the trials and tribulations of life at *Fawlty Towers* and they consider themselves satisfied customers. Indeed, loyal to Basil through thick and thin, Miss Tibbs and Miss Gatsby are the only guests who defend the hotel when it comes under American assault during 'Waldorf Salad'. The comic refinement that Renée Roberts and Gilly Flower brought to their roles makes them a fondly remembered part of the series, while their presence adds an important degree of heart and soul to the terrifying tornado that is Basil Fawlty.

In an interesting touch of television intertextuality, both Roberts and Flower were cast in the fourth series of *Only Fools and Horses* in 1985. They appeared in one episode each, the first and second of the series, and played the taxing role of Old Lady. Clearly writer John Sullivan had an affection and knowledge of the classic situation comedy that pre-dated his own popular series.

Basil humours Miss Tibbs and Miss Gatsby in 'The Builders' as they seem rather more excited about his weekend away with Sybil than he does – 'Well, it's only Paignton.'

GUEST STARS

'You ponce in here expecting to be waited on hand and foot, well I'm trying to run a hotel here.'
Basil Fawlty

WHILE the pivotal characters in *Fawlty Towers* are unquestionably Basil, Sybil, Manuel and Polly, many other actors were required to create the basic premise of each episode, fleshing out the comic business in the scripts, and providing straight men and women opposite whom the principals could explore the extremes that their characters could reach under pressure.

Here is an A–Z celebration of those largely unsung people who ventured through the portals of *Fawlty Towers* and survived – in the main – the hotel from hell.

TREVOR ADAMS

Alan, the grinning charmer in the episode 'The Wedding Party', clearly gets Basil's goat. His easy acceptance of the steamy atmosphere that overlays the episode is in stark contrast with Basil's repressed prudishness. This unfavourable comparison makes Basil all the more determined to thwart Alan and his giggly companion's perfectly natural desire for a double bed.

Adams, who played Alan, had been part of the 1971 sketch show *What Are You Doing After the Show?* with Hilary Pritchard and Rob Buckman. Following his *Fawlty Towers* appearance in 1976, he was cast as the irritating yes-man, Tony Webster, in *The Fall and Rise of Reginald Perrin*.

ELIZABETH BENSON

Elizabeth Benson is one of only two people to have chalked up the rather distinguished achievement of appearing in *Fawlty Towers* as two completely different characters. (Terence Conoley is the other.) In the first series' episode 'Gourmet Night' she is the fiery and rather repellent Mrs Heath, continually cooing over her obnoxious and spoilt son (Tony Page) and barking insults at her henpecked husband (Jeffrey Segal). In 'The Kipper and the Corpse' episode in the second series, she returned as the more controlled and timid character Mrs White, who, with her husband (Richard Davies), is shocked to find a dead body and a screaming old lady in their hotel room wardrobe.

NORMAN BIRD

Born in 1924, Norman Bird is one of the most prolific character actors of the pre-war era. He appeared in literally dozens of British films following his big-screen debut in the Alastair Sim chiller *An Inspector Calls* in 1954, but found national fame on television when he starred as the geography teacher, S.A. Smallpiece, opposite Jimmy Edwards in the first series of *Whack-O!* in 1956. He affectionately refers to himself as 'the man with the cardigan' owing to his many domestic roles as an ineffectual and henpecked husband. Bird's work on film has spanned everything from cops and robbers (*The League of Gentlemen*) and union politics (*The Angry Silence*) to rural drama (*Whistle Down the Wind*) and satire (*The Rise and Rise of Michael Rimmer*). Throughout the 1960s Bird enjoyed a string of supporting parts in some of the most influential productions of the decade, featuring in the Dirk Bogarde film *Victim*, the Peter Cushing bank robbery thriller *Cash On Demand* and Sidney Lumet's prisoner of war flick *The Hill*.

He returned to situation comedy in the 1965 show *It's Not Me – It's Them!*, later appearing in *Miss Jones and Son*, *Up the Workers* and *Worzel Gummidge*. In 1973 Bird was cast as Inspector Street in Barry Took's Holmesian *Comedy Playhouse* episode 'Elementary, My Dear Watson' with John Cleese as the great detective. When producer Douglas Argent was casting the second series of *Fawlty Towers*, he had the chance to reunite the two. Bird was the perfect choice for the mild-mannered hotel guest Mr Arrad in 'Waldorf Salad'. Playing opposite the feisty Stella Tanner as his wife, Bird is stoical and uncomplaining. Kept waiting for half an hour for his food and finally given the incorrect order,

Mr Arrad would rather keep quiet than risk the ire of the bombastic Basil. He is the archetype of the mild-mannered everyman that Bird had played for a quarter of a century.

BRUCE BOA

It was in 1977 that Bruce Boa, playing a typically straight-talking American, landed his first starring role in a British sitcom, *Yanks Go Home*. Produced and directed by Eric Prytherch, the series dealt with the trials and tribulations of life in an English village after the Americans set up camp in 1942. Also in the cast was Norman Bird, and a couple of years later both actors were reunited in the *Fawlty Towers* episode 'Waldorf Salad'. Boa played Mr Hamilton, an American visitor who becomes more and more outraged and ouspoken as Basil's increasingly ludicrous explanations of the poor service go beyond comprehensibility. The American complains about the foul British weather, the difficulty of driving 'on the wrong side of the road' and the impossibility of obtaining a waldorf salad and a screwdriver cocktail. Boa's explosive comic talents were used again in the 1981 science fiction comedy *Astronauts* written by Graeme Garden and Bill Oddie. Boa played Beadle, a frantic Mission Control worker, and the only source of contact for the space-bound 'Sky-Lab'. His film roles include two stints with the US embassy: *The Omen* (1976) and *Carry On Emmannuelle* (1978).

RICHARD CALDICOT

Another of the most familiar and best-loved character actors in the business, Caldicot cornered the market in supercilious butlers, shifty-looking policemen and bamboozled figures of military authority. His dulcet tones and slow-burn bursts of anger were captured at their best in the long-running BBC Radio comedy *The Navy Lark*, which endured from 1959 until 1977. He also joined forces with the series' creator, Laurie Wyman, for the similarly nautical TV show, *HMS Paradise*, and starred opposite Jim Dale in the children's comedy *Pet Pals*. Throughout his career, Caldicot notched up dozens of stage and film appearances, from Shakespeare to slapstick. But apart from *The Navy Lark*, it was television that secured him his finest roles. He played the befuddled Councillor Cooper in the 1977 Thora Hird comedy *The Boys and Mrs B*, later joined the cast of the Lorraine Chase series *The Other 'Arf*

Claire Nielson (Mrs Hamilton) looks on as her husband (Bruce Boa) clashes with Basil in 'Waldorf Salad' – 'You know what fella – if this was back in the States I wouldn't board my dog here.'

and happily stooged for many comedians from Roy Hudd to Ron Moody.

In 1970 Caldicot made a guest appearance in the first series of *The Goodies*, barking with military fervour as the beauty of the countryside is lost to a nuclear waste-dump.

He again embodied upper-class pomposity when he played the jovial Mr Twitchen – that's pronounced 'Twy-Chin' – in the first series *Fawlty Towers* episode 'Gourmet Night'. Initially cheerful and chatty, he becomes increasingly uncomfortable with Basil's angst and painful attempts to avoid pronouncing his name (his fellow diner has a facial tic).

Caldicot's professionalism and experience shine through his portrayal of this minor but beautifully acted figure of Torquay high society.

'How very *au fait* of you to come to our little culinary *soirée* this evening.' Basil welcomes the Twitchens to his 'Gourmet Night'.

KEN CAMPBELL

The unpredictable comic genius of Ken Campbell first burst into the public's attention in the insane *Ken Campbell Roadshow* in the late 1960s. His style was madcap and frenzied, and his act featured the classic 'ferret-down-the-trousers' routine. Among his team were future household names Bob Hoskins and Sylvester McCoy. Indeed, Campbell was on the shortlist when his old friend McCoy was cast as *Doctor Who* in 1987. According to McCoy, 'Ken would have made a better villain. Maybe if we'd carried on doing *Doctor Who*, I would have tried to get my mate in it. He would have been brilliant as another Master or a Rani.' However, apart from his regular role as the wild-eyed and aggressive Fred Johnson opposite Warren Mitchell's Alf Garnett in *In Sickness and Health*, Campbell seems to have shunned mainstream entertainment. He prefers to dedicate himself to experimental theatre. He has written several films and stage plays including *One Night I Danced with Mr Dalton* (which cast John Alderton and Pauline Collins together for the first time) and *The Madness Museum* (in which Campbell himself plays the owner of an asylum) and has presented a couple of Channel 4 documentaries about quantum physics and philosophy. In 1979, he appeared in the Amnesty International Benefit concert *The Secret Policeman's Ball*, with a cast including Peter Cook, Terry Jones and John Cleese.

That same year, Campbell was cast in *Fawlty Towers* as the sarcastic and annoying Roger of

'The Anniversary'. Stretching Basil's tolerance to the limit, Campbell's non-stop cracks and stage-whispered observations created one of the most memorable one-off characterizations in the series. A decade later, when Cleese filmed an advertisement for 'Auntie Beeb' – 'What Have the BBC Ever Done For Us?' – Campbell was signed up to stagger out of a pub toilet and mutter: 'Alternative comedy!' He remains one of the most inventive talents in British comedy today.

TERENCE CONOLEY

A familiar face in British stage and television comedy, Terence Conoley, with Elizabeth Benson, is one of only two guest actors to appear in more than one episode of *Fawlty Towers* in two completely different roles. In the very first episode, 'A Touch of Class', he is the balding guest continually moved on in favour of the all-important Lord Melbury, and spends most of the last five minutes yelling his bar order: 'A gin and orange, a lemon squash and a scotch and water, please.' As producer/director John Howard Davies remembers: 'Conoley's was a wonderful piece of acting because he had to come in late and deal with absolute reality. It's very difficult to play small parts like that and have the amount of impact that he had.'

In 1979 he returned for a role in 'Waldorf Salad', this time with hair, as the equally disgruntled guest Mr Johnston, with June Ellis playing his wife.

JAMES COSSINS

An expert at playing slightly squiffy majors and dubious second-hand car dealers, Cossins first made his mark on stage, but went on to perform in many films, including *The Anniversary* with Bette Davis and *Death Line* with Christopher Lee. On television he enlivened many a situation comedy, playing alongside George Cole and Gwen Watford in *Don't Forget to Write*, Brian Murphy in *L for Lester* and Patricia Routledge and Patricia Hayes in *Marjorie and Men*. Cossins

OPPOSITE: Roger interrogates Basil as to Sybil's true whereabouts in 'The Anniversary'.

RIGHT: 'I'm afraid most of the people we get in here don't know a Bordeaux from a claret.' Basil demonstrates his appreciation for the 'boudoir' of the grape in 'The Hotel Inspectors'.

was then cast as Major Andrews in the Richard Briers comedy *All in Good Faith*. The producer was John Howard Davies who, a decade earlier, had used Cossins in *Fawlty Towers* as the red herring, Mr Walt, in 'The Hotel Inspectors'. Unimpressed but unperturbed by Basil's ignorance of fine wines, and choking back his amazement at Manuel's incompetence, Cossins is finally flabbergasted when accosted by a desperate Basil over his entry in the all-important 'book'. He is also involved in the earlier scene when Basil, bickering with the infuriating Mr Hutchison over the writing on a map, turns to Mr Walt for verification, demanding, 'Does it say Boff, or does it say Poff? There, it's a P, isn't it?' 'I suppose so.' replies Mr Walt. '*P. Off!*' Basil re-emphasizes. 'I beg your pardon!' barks the outraged Walt.

BRENDA COWLING

Although best known as Mrs Lipton in the sitcom *You Rang M'Lord*, Brenda Cowling has many other credits to her name. She first gained public recognition as Gwen Notley in the 1974 sitcom *Good Girl*, while on film she became a prized part of the *Carry On...* series as the bossy matron in *Carry On Girls*, and enjoying a frantic caravan-camp moment in *Carry On Behind*. It was in 1975 that Cowling joined the cast of *Fawlty Towers*, playing the starchy sister who treats Sybil Fawlty's ingrowing toenail in 'The Germans'. Humiliated by a concussed and out-of-control Basil for her brisk and patronizing manner, she is only shocked into silence when he remarks, 'My God, you're ugly aren't you?' adding, 'You need a plastic surgeon, dear, not a doctor,' for good measure.

Brenda Cowling played the over-officious hospital sister in 'The Germans'.

BERNARD CRIBBINS

A comedy veteran of 40 years' standing, Bernard Cribbins has notched up some fine performances on stage, film and television. First achieving recognition as a popular revue star of the 1950s and 1960s, he made his big-screen debut in the 1957 wartime drama *Yangtse Incident* and became a surprise recording star with hits such as 'Right Said Fred' and 'Hole in the Ground', although Cribbins was reluctant to take his singing career seriously: 'The songs were amazing accidents. I want to be judged as a comedy actor and that's about the most serious thing you can be.'

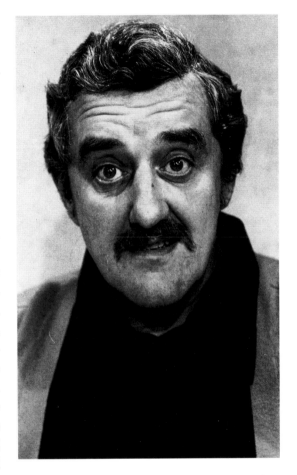

On film Cribbins has sparred with the best of them, appearing with Norman Wisdom in *The Girl on the Boat* (1961), Peter Sellers in *Two-Way Stretch* (1962) and Terry-Thomas in *The Mouse On the Moon* (1963). During a 30-year association with the *Carry On...* series, he chalked up leading roles in the nautical adventure *Carry On Jack* and the espionage romp *Carry On Spying* in 1964. Almost three decades later, he was recalled for the ill-fated reprise *Carry On Columbus*. Cribbins starred opposite Peter Cushing in the second *Doctor Who* feature film, *Daleks – Invasion Earth 2150AD,* and sang and danced the immortal *Watch the Birdie* routine with Tommy Steele and Sid James in *Tommy the Toreador*. Under the direction of Lionel Jeffries, Cribbins gave a satisfying film performance as the kindly stationmaster in *The Railway Children*. By way of contrast he also played the bossy pub landlord in Alfred Hitchcock's *Frenzy* (1972).

On television, Cribbins has always appeared to great effect, but it was in *Fawlty Towers*, as the annoying and punctilious Mr Hutchison in 'The Hotel Inspectors', that he created his best remembered small-screen character. His insistence on every imaginable extra, his yearning for a particular 'televisual feast' and his complaints about shoddy treatment in the dining room, provide some of the best moments in the series. The eventual revelation that he is a spoon salesman rather than a hotel inspector sets the stage for Basil to launch a frenzied attack on this exasperating guest. Mr Hutchison's enraged retaliation is an almost shockingly violent moment in a series not known for its mildness.

'Is there something we can get you, Mr Hutchison? A tea cosy for your pepper pot, perhaps?'

MICHAEL CRONIN

Who could forget the bumbling cowboy builder Spud Lurphy, the 'hideous orang-utan' portrayed by Michael Cronin in 'The Builders'. The actor later delighted a generation of young viewers as the sports master in *Grange Hill*. Cronin played the popular teacher Mr Geoff 'Bullet' Baxter in the children's soap from 1979 to 1986.

ALLAN CUTHBERTSON

Born in Perth, Western Australia, Allan Cuthbertson made his British stage debut as the young male lead in *Romeo and Juliet* in 1947. He went on to carve out a solid career on stage, television and film, often being cast as officious military types or perturbed civil servants.

It was but a short step to becoming a comic's stooge, and he played the straight man to many well-known names, including Sheila Hancock, John Le Mesurier, Tommy Cooper, Morecambe and Wise and Frankie Howerd. His success as cold-hearted authority figures led Terry Jones and Michael Palin to cast Cuthbertson as the frightfully proper Major Daintry in *Ripping Yarns*, and he appeared as the po-faced Mr Horrobin in Palin's bittersweet film of young love, *East of Ipswich*.

'Oh, sorry! Didn't see you down there. Don't get up.' – The 'Gourmet Night' gets off to a fine start as Basil insults the first of the evening's guests.

Around the same time, he was recruited to *Fawlty Towers* to play the bellowing military figure of Colonel Hall in the episode 'Gourmet Night', a masterpiece of explosive rage. Twitching with anger and possessing absolutely no sense of humour, the Colonel is one establishment figure too authoritarian for Basil to placate. In fact, we are moved to sympathy for Basil when he tries to ingratiate himself by recalling their last meeting and is brutally rebuffed. Cuthbertson died in February 1988 at the age of 67.

CLAIRE DAVENPORT

A larger than life character actress who worked with the great and good of British comedy, Claire Davenport was the perfect vehicle for humour based on innuendo, farce and sometimes downright smut. She appeared in several sex comedies of the late 1970s, such as *Adventures of a Plumber's Mate* and *Carry On Emmannuelle*. One of her first sitcom appearances was in 1963 as Myrtle in *The Rag Trade*, with Peter Jones and Reg Varney. Other film credits include the 1980 production of *The Elephant Man* with John Hurt, and an appearance as a denizen of Jabba the Hut's palace in *Return of the Jedi*. In 1975 she joined *Fawlty Towers* to play the rather pompous and confused Mrs Wilson in the fire drill half of 'The Germans'.

RICHARD DAVIES

One of the best-known Welshmen in British television comedy, Richard Davies has made a career out of Celtic moaning and wide-eyed frustration. He is perhaps most fondly remembered as the jovial maths and science teacher, Mr Price, in *Please, Sir!*, a huge sitcom hit in the 1960s. He went on to make his mark in *Rule Britannia!* and *Oh, No – It's Selwyn Froggitt*, but rarely changed his characterization: his portrayal of bewildered disbelief could turn to flamboyant joy in a matter of minutes, but a certain Welsh dourness was always ready to surface when needed. He enjoyed his brief moment of *Fawlty Towers* fame in 'The Kipper and the Corpse'. As Mr White, he earnestly survived life at *Fawlty Towers*, doggedly trying to get past Polly's none-too-subtle delaying tactics and ultimately finding a dead body and a deranged Miss Tibbs in his bedroom cupboard. In 1982, Davies and Cleese were reunited in *Whoops Apocalypse*, which cast Davies as the Chancellor of the Exchequer.

Basil and Manuel do their best to distract Mr White (Richard Davies) in 'The Kipper and the Corpse'.

ROBIN ELLIS

Playing the flashy and laid-back Danny Brown in the very first episode of *Fawlty Towers*, 'A Touch of Class', Ellis is a profound irritant to the snobbish Basil. Easy and self-assured, Danny breezes into the hotel, every bit the working-class boy made good, and proceeds to chat up

117

the unimpressed Polly right under the nose of the fuming Basil. Confident, casual and carefree – in fact, everything that Basil isn't – Danny adds insult to injury by being loaded (a classy white sports car is parked outside), having a glamorous job (with a special police investigation) and, most galling of all, speaking Spanish better than Basil. With Danny able to confound all his prejudices, Basil can only resort to unfounded hatred and schoolyard name-calling. Ellis is great in the role, and went on to star as Poldark, amongst many other TV parts.

Poldark star Robin Ellis turns up as the charismatic, Spanish-speaking undercover police officer Danny Brown in 'A Touch of Class'.

SABINA FRANKLYN

The attractive actress with a flair for comedy sprang to fame as Jacqui Rush in the situation comedy *Keep It in the Family* from 1980. Sharing a downstairs flat with her sister (played by Stacy Dorning), the unthreatening but amusing scripts kept the nation laughing until 1983. Two years later she starred with Christopher Strauli in *Full House*. Her first foray into the genre had been in the very last episode of *Fawlty Towers*, 'Basil the Rat', in 1979. In this she played Quentina, who enjoyed the fun and games with the offending rodent.

YVONNE GILAN

Embodying continental sophistication and charm, Yvonne Gilan played the flirtatious Mrs Peignoir in 'The Wedding Party'. Basil is, at first, clearly a little entranced by her, though perhaps rather bewildered that she appears to like him too.

By the end of the episode, fear of Sybil has overcome any attraction he might feel for the French woman, and he is seen hissing through his bedroom door, 'Shut up, will you, you silly great tart! Go away! My wife will hear us.' 'This is your wife,' Sybil replies.

Gilan was an experienced stage actress and revue star, having appeared in Alan Bennett's 1966 sketch series *On the Margin*. Her son is the television critic A.A. Gill.

ELSPET GRAY

One of the country's finest farceurs, and married to another (Brian Rix), Elspet Gray appeared opposite her husband in the early 1960s series *Dial RIX*, which also featured Andrew Sachs.

In the late 1970s she was a regular as wife number two in the Patrick Cargill comedy *The Many Wives of Patrick*, and co-starred with Felicity Kendal in the 1981 series *Solo*. In 1983 she played the Queen in the first *Blackadder*

'You're **two** doctors? Well, how did you become two doctors? … I mean, did you take the exams twice?' Sybil and the Abbotts stare in bemusement at Basil.

series, *The Black Adder*. In the second series of *Fawlty Towers* she was cast as 'Mrs ... I'm Sorry ... Dr Abbott' in 'The Psychiatrist', thoroughly bemused by Basil's antics as he tries hard to demonstrate his normality to her psychiatrist husband.

MICHAEL GWYNN

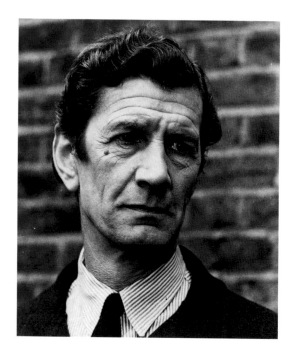

Playing the corrupt charmer Lord Melbury in 'A Touch of Class', Michael Gwynn was the very first major guest star in the series. His upper-class persona exposes Basil's underlying predilection for forelock-tugging sycophancy, never happier than when fawning on the élite. His sharp exit near the end of the episode, at Basil's wrathful reference to 'bricks', is one of the funniest moments of the show.

Gwynn had made a name for himself in a wide variety of British films from the early 1950s, appearing with Frankie Howerd in *The Runaway Bus*, playing the sympathetic monster in *The Revenge of Frankenstein* and cropping up in the science fiction thriller *Village of the Damned*. Sadly, Gwynn died just one year after playing Lord Melbury, at the age of 60.

NICKY HENSON

One of those rare actors who enlivens any production with his mere presence, Nicky Henson, son of comedian Leslie Henson, enjoyed early popularity in British horror films such as *Witchfinder General*, *Psychomania* (where his emergence from the grave on a motorbike has gone down as one of the most bizarre moments in British film history) and *Vampira*. In 1976 he recreated the role made famous by Albert Finney when he played the cocky hero

in *The Bawdy Adventures of Tom Jones*. He went on to play a string of optimistic bighead roles on television, acquiring various comedy parts on the way. The best of these were in *Anyone for Dennis*, *The Frost Report* and *The Wrong Man*, and his lead role (taking over from Kenneth Cranham) in *Shine On, Harvey Moon*.

Henson's contribution to *Fawlty Towers* came in the episode 'The Psychiatrist', where his manly display of chest hair, off-hand condemnation of the Torquay attractions and flamboyant charm with the opposite sex act like a red rag to a bull on Basil. Sybil's all-too-apparent fascination with Henson's Mr Johnson echoes Basil's own weakness for Mrs Peignoir, but he is blissfully unaware of any parallel. Henson's patent lack of interest in Sybil's inane banter about her mother's phobias is inspired, and the spiritual meaning of his collection of medallions – decoration to him, mystic charms to her – reveals his fundamental shallowness. The medallion man is a satisfyingly awful stereotype, played to perfection by Henson.

Basil reiterates the importance of the hotel's no-visitor rule.

BETTY HUNTLEY-WRIGHT

In the early 1960s Betty Huntley-Wright flirted with situation comedy stardom when she played Lillian Broadbent in *Bulldog Breed* with Donald Churchill, Amanda Barrie, Peter Butterworth and *Fawlty Towers* guest star Geoffrey Palmer. Later, in 1964, she appeared with Lance Percival in the Comedy Playhouse episode, 'The Mate Market'. It was in 1975, however, that she was to appear in her most high-profile show, when she was cast as Richard Caldicot's bemused wife, Mrs Twitchen, in 'Gourmet Night'.

DAVID KELLY

One of the unsung heroes of British situation comedy, David Kelly's many performances have enriched and enlivened numerous shows. None, however, comes close to his single appearance in *Fawlty Towers*. Although his character, the cowboy builder Mr O'Reilly, is mentioned during a telephone conversation in 'A Touch of Class', it isn't until 'The Builders' that he appears on screen. Already established as an incompetent worker by Sybil's poor opinion of him, we never really believe his jovial, optimistic claims, and it's likely that Basil doesn't either. But hope triumphs over experience and the awful consequences unfold. We watch, fascinated, as his roguish assertion that he likes 'a woman with spirit' dooms him to a merciless verbal and physical battering from Sybil.

Kelly had sprung to fame when cast as Cousin Enda in the late 1960s series *Me Mammy*. The popularity of the piece led him to be teamed once more with Milo O'Shea for the 1972 series *Tales From A Lazy Acre*. In the wake of *Fawlty Towers*, Kelly was offered the regular role of Albert Riddle in *Robin's Nest*. Albert, the cheerful ex-jailbird with only one arm, who held the position of washer-upper in Richard O'Sullivan's restaurant was a great success. The spectre of his *Fawlty Towers* character remained so strong that when Peter Learmouth wrote *Cowboys*, a series about a firm of dodgy builders in 1980, Kelly was immediately cast as Wobbly Ron. Other television work included *Oh Father!* with Derek Nimmo, *Whoops Apocalypse* with John Cleese and *Slinger's Day* with Bruce Forsyth. More recently, Kelly starred with Ian Bannen in the comedy film *Waking Ned*, an Ealing-style fantasy that allowed Kelly to present his familiar self on a much larger canvas.

DIANA KING

The queen mother of British situation comedies, Diana King was the perfect maternal figure in countless small-screen roles. Her earliest outing was as Richard Briers' mother in *Marriage Lines*, but she also cropped up as Captain Peacock's prissy wife in *Are You Being Served?* and later played Hannah Gordon's mother in *My Wife Next Door*. Other television credits included *Cuffy* with Bernard Cribbins, *Bachelor Father* with Ian Carmichael, *Sharon and Elsie* with Brigit Forsyth and *You're Only Young Twice* with Peggy Mount and Pat Coombs. In between times she appeared in *Fawlty Towers* as the pink-hatted Mrs Rachel Lloyd in 'The Wedding Party', utterly bewildered by Basil's attempts to keep her husband's supposed infidelity out of sight.

'He's just having a lie down.' – Basil reassures Mrs Lloyd that Manuel is simply enjoying a siesta in 'The Wedding Party'.

GEORGE LEE

Only one actor returned for a second guest appearance as a recurring character, and that was laconic George Lee who played a bemused delivery man. In the episode 'The Builders' he appears as a nameless worker who tries to deliver a gnome to the hotel while Manuel is temporarily in charge. To his annoyance, Manuel attempts to book the gnome into Room 16. In 'Communication Problems' George Lee returned as Mr Kerr, presumably the same delivery man, this time delivering a valuable vase and a glove containing Mrs Richards' missing money from the unusually diversely stocked shop he works for.

CHARLES McKEOWN

McKeown, a long-standing collaborator with the *Monty Python* team, joined *Fawlty Towers* for a joke that didn't quite come off. John Cleese had long wanted to wreak revenge on Richard Ingrams, *Private Eye* scribe and creator of the *Oldie* magazine, for his vitriolic reviews of *Monty Python*.

His original idea was to name the soon-to-be dead character in 'The Kipper and the Corpse' Mr Ignoramus, a none-too-subtle play on the name 'Ingrams'. However, cold feet at the last minute made Cleese change the name to Mr Leeman – after the head waiter of the Savoy Grill, who had originally given Cleese the idea about removing 'stiffs' from the building without other guests noticing. Still, the name Ingrams does crop up, albeit briefly, as a guest played by McKeown who has no importance within the plot, and is only present to make the link between the name and the cold fish of the episode's title.

McKeown's other work with the Pythons includes *Life of Brian*, Gilliam's *The Adventures of Baron Munchausen* and Palin's *American Friends*. On television he played Mr Hargreaves in Palin's 1987 play *East of Ipswich*.

ANDRE MARANNE

French actor André Maranne as the Fawltys' restaurant-owning friend, planning the 'Gourmet Night' with Basil and Sybil.

The accomplished chef and restaurant owner who comes to Basil's aid in 'Gourmet Night' is the calm eye in the storm. It is he who provides the ill-fated duck and emergency sauces to try to salvage *Fawlty Towers'* foray into *haute cuisine*. André Maranne gives a controlled supporting performance that contrasts beautifully with Basil's spiralling anxiety. Maranne's other television credits have included *Doctor Who*, where he was memorably attacked by a Cyberman in 'The Moonbase'. On film he is probably best remembered as François, the uneasy and bemused assistant to Inspector Clouseau in the *Pink Panther* films.

CLAIRE NIELSON

As Mrs Hamilton, the refined British wife of Bruce Boa's impatient American in the episode 'Waldorf Salad', Claire Nielson is the person whom Basil ill-advisedly takes aside to condemn the loud-mouthed behaviour of the American. His embarrassment when she reveals her connection to the disparaged man, and his subsequent attempts to ingratiate himself are squirmingly awful. We feel that Mrs Hamilton must be congratulating herself on escaping the English, if this is a representative specimen.

Nielson's sitcom career after *Fawlty Towers* embraced some interesting near-misses: she played Grace Hills in the 1981 Michele Dotrice series *Chintz*, and in 1991 played Christopher Godwin's wife in the ballroom dancing comedy *Taking the Floor*.

GEOFFREY PALMER

A gift to British comedy writers, Geoffrey Palmer has graced some of the best and worst of shows, but has always given a peerless performance. From 1976 he played the military-minded Jimmy in the weird world of Reggie Perrin, where his flights of fancy and manic battle plans with a wary Leonard Rossiter were among the high points of the show. He then excelled as the dour dentist Ben Parkinson alongside Wendy Craig in Carla Lane's *Butterflies*, which ran from 1978 until 1983. He was then cast by David Nobbs as the crusty Harry Truscott in *Fairly Secret Army*, and by David Renwick as Harry Stringer in the first series of *Hot Metal*. A particular high spot in his career came in 1989, when he appeared in a cameo role in the final episode of *Blackadder Goes Forth*.

From 1992 Palmer played Lionel Hardcastle in the endearing sitcom *As Time Goes By* and later teamed up with his co-star, Judi Dench, in several James Bond films. In 2001 he played the disgruntled father of Marcus Brigstocke in Simon Nye's *The Savages*.

In between times, Palmer brought his familiar touch of world-weariness to *Fawlty Towers* in 'The Kipper and the Corpse'. As the lugubrious Dr Price, driven to extreme lengths to get some sausages for breakfast, he witnesses Basil trying to hide a dead body. The comic business that ensues relies heavily on the contrast between Basil's panic and the doctor's cool pragmatism. Palmer worked with John Cleese again in 1982's *Whoops Apocalypse* and, together with Prunella Scales, in the *Look At the State We're In* series.

LUAN PETERS

In 'The Psychiatrist', innocent Australian Raylene Miles is subjected to Basil's unintentional harassment, as his plans to expose Mr Johnson's clandestine guest land him in ever deeper water with Sybil. Groped, smeared with black paint, her room invaded, she could be forgiven for feeling somewhat uneasy in the presence of the hotel owner.

The blonde actress who played the Australian guest was a familiar face in British entertainment during the 1970s. Among Luan Peters' credits was the Hammer Horror film *Twins of Evil*, and in 1977, just before her appearance in *Fawlty Towers*, she played a stripper in the Thora Hird comedy *The Boys and Mrs B*.

John Cleese, Luan Peters and Prunella Scales in rehearsal for the 'groping scene' in 'The Psychiatrist'.

CONRAD PHILLIPS

Although he carved out an impressive career on stage and screen during the 1940s and '50s, Conrad Phillips achieved greatest fame for playing William Tell in the popular TV series that ran from 1958 to 1966. The role, however, proved to be something of a curse. Like Richard Greene with Robin Hood, he could never quite escape his small-screen persona. He kept busy with television roles in *Sutherland's Law*, *Heidi* and *The Newcomers*, and also worked opposite Morecambe and Wise, Dick Emery and Ronnie Corbett. In 1975 he joined *Fawlty Towers* to play the urbane Mr Lloyd in 'The Wedding Party'. Throughout the farcical antics of the episode, Phillips gives a low-key performance that serves to point up the insanity around him. Now enjoying life in semi-retirement in Normandy, Phillips has made one return to television – playing Stefan, the grey-haired mentor to none other than William Tell in the international co-production *Crossbow*.

STEVE PLYTAS

Expert at playing fiery, exotic continentals, Steve Plytas was perfectly cast as the passionate Greek chef, Kurt, in 'Gourmet Night'. While preparing the evening's specialities, his character's penchant for the 'cute' Manuel goes unrequited and he hits the bottle to drown his sorrows. Under his increasingly unstable stewardship, the kitchen becomes a disaster area.

Plytas had, in fact, been part of an earlier situation-comedy era when he played a gutter journalist in the 1959 children's series *The Young Lady from London*. His sporadic film work included *Ooh …You Are Awful* (1972), playing a conman victim, and *Carry On Emmannuelle* (1978) in which he was cast as an Arabian diplomat seduced by Suzanne Danielle.

MAVIS PUGH

Fondly remembered as a character actress who specialized in slightly dotty ladies of a certain vintage, Mavis Pugh became well known when she was cast as the eccentric Lady Lavender in

You Rang M'Lord, a parody of *Upstairs, Downstairs*. A decade earlier she had appeared in *Fawlty Towers* as the fussy, dog-loving old dear, Mrs Chase, in 'The Kipper and the Corpse'.

DEREK ROYLE

The perfect dead weight in *Fawlty Towers*, Derek Royle, an experienced comedy actor on stage and television, landed the role of the ill-fated Mr Leeman in the second series' episode 'The Kipper and the Corpse'. Preoccupied and uncertain from the outset, he is assailed by relentless helpfulness from Sybil and relentless rudeness from Basil, which combine to make his final moments on earth something of a trial.

While Royle effectively conveys a sense of distraction in Mr Leeman, his performance stands out for his ability to play possum and

keep a straight face as his 'dead body' is lugged about the hotel like an unwanted sack of potatoes. It's a fine if somewhat limited performance, and makes the bickering of Cleese and Sachs and the incredulous monologues of Geoffrey Palmer all the funnier.

Royle had, in fact, starred in his own sitcom, a children's series called *Hogg's Back*, in 1975. In 1989 he replaced the late Jack Haig as the 'master of disguise', Monsieur Leclerc, in the wartime romp, *'Allo, 'Allo*. Sadly, Royle himself died after playing the part for just one series.

A rehearsal shot of guest star Derek Royle who spends most of 'The Kipper and the Corpse' episode being dragged around the hotel as the dead guest Mr Leeman.

JOAN SANDERSON

Unforgettable as the deaf harridan Mrs Richards in 'Communication Problems', Joan Sanderson's never-smiling, foul-tempered guest was one of Basil's most sustained irritants. Her deafness proves a wonderful comic device, allowing Basil to utter a stream of enjoyably candid and inventive insults. Her complaint about the lack of view from her bedroom window, for

The Major's memory plays up as Basil struggles to convince Mrs Richards that the money is his in 'Communication Problems'.

example, prompts Basil to launch into one of his most famous tirades: 'Well … may I ask what you were expecting to see out of a Torquay hotel bedroom window? Sydney Opera House, perhaps? The hanging gardens of Babylon? Herds of wildebeest sweeping majestically …'

Sanderson's career included many performances as a frosty-faced ogress, but the one that brought her fame was the starchy Doris Ewell in the 1960s series *Please, Sir!* Other television work included shows with Les Dawson, the religious comedy series *All Gas and Gaiters* and *Ripping Yarns*. Her film credits were very diverse, everything from *The Muppet Movie* to Alan Bennett's biopic of Joe Orton, *Prick Up Your Ears*, while on stage she was excellent in *Habeas Corpus* (with Andrew Sachs) and the Thatcherite satire *Anyone For Denis?* In 1986 she appeared in the sitcom *Full House* with Christopher Strauli, taking over from fellow *Fawlty Towers* guest Diana King as the hapless hero's mother. Sanderson's last role, on radio and television, was as Prunella Scales' mother in *After Henry*, and capitalized on all the qualities for which she had become best known. Her death, shortly after completing work on the fourth TV series, was a sad loss. Playwright Alan Bennett remembered her as a fine purveyor of comedy.

JEFFREY SEGAL

A pebble-glassed character actor with a skill for henpecked husbands and ineffectual civil servants, Jeffrey Segal played the hapless Mr Heath in 'Gourmet Night', with Elizabeth Benson as his domineering wife. In 1980 he played Arthur Perkins in the Harry Worth series *Oh Happy Band!* However, Segal is perhaps best remembered as the long-suffering neighbour in the cult children's comedy *Rentaghost*, which ran from 1976 to 1984.

DAVID SIMEON

The very first actor to play a guest at *Fawlty Towers* was David Simeon, who appeared as the inconvenienced but apologetic Mr Mackenzie, made late by the non-appearance of his requested alarm call. Simeon went on to appear in lacklustre situation comedies, including *Kelly's Eye* with Matthew Kelly and *A Small Problem* with ex-Young One Christopher Ryan. The following year he played the clerk of the court in *A Fish Called Wanda*.

UNA STUBBS

In the course of her 50-year career, Una Stubbs has appeared alongside many comic talents, including Ron Moody and Victoria Wood, but it was as an icon of the swinging '60s that she found her greatest fame. In 1962 Stubbs had sung and danced her way into the

nation's affections as part of Cliff Richard's gang in *Summer Holiday*. She went on to play the whining, hard-done-by Rita, daughter of Alf Garnett, in *Till Death Us Do Part* from 1965 to 1975, and she reprised the role in 1985 in the spin-off series *In Sickness and Health*. With Warren Mitchell, Dandy Nicholls and her man, the 'scouse git' Anthony Booth, Stubbs formed part of an embodiment of the working-class family.

For her guest appearance in *Fawlty Towers* she was cast as Alice, the rather timid wife of Roger (Ken Campbell) in 'The Anniversary'. Sweet and ineffectual, Alice could not have been a greater contrast to the character that went on to make her an anti-heroine to a generation of children. As Aunt Sally she scoffed cakes and dished out insults to Jon Pertwee's loveable scarecrow in *Worzel Gummidge*. Towards the end of the '80s Stubbs and Pertwee were reunited in Australia for the hit spin-off *Worzel Gummidge Down Under*.

STELLA TANNER

One of comedy's unsung heroines, Stella Tanner enlivened many a situation comedy and sketch series with her hard-nosed, acidic performances. None were more so than her *Fawlty Towers* appearance as Mrs Arrad in the episode 'Waldorf Salad'. Here we find her in full flow bulling her husband (Norman Bird) and outfacing Basil's pathetic excuses. Tanner had first come to prominence as Olive in the third series of *The Rag Trade*, in 1963. In 1968 she played Mrs Green in the comedy *Thingumybob* and in 1975 appeared as Vera Caplan in *My Son Reuben*. Perhaps her finest moments came in the anarchic company of Spike Milligan, where her performances provided the perfect foil for his surreal humour. Tanner appeared with Milligan in *Q6*, *Q7* and *Q8* from 1975 until 1979.

APRIL WALKER

As the blonde raver, Jean Wilson, April Walker's giggling performance in 'The Wedding Party' brought out Basil's puritanical streak, leading to door-banging, 'couple-swapping' farce. Walker went on to appear with Les Dawson in *The Dawson Watch* and with Eric Sykes in *Rhubarb, Rhubarb*, before landing the role of Virginia in *Wyatt's Watchdog* in 1988.

ANN WAY

This diminutive British comedy actress excels at playing bewildered and nervous ladies, not least the tittering Mrs Hall in the episode 'Gourmet Night'. Her diplomatic, if timid, approach to the appalling service is in sharp contrast to the anger of her husband (played by Allan Cuthbertson). In 1970 Way had enjoyed a brief association with the *Carry On* team when she was cast as part of the eccentric Grubb family, alongside Joan Hickson, Imogen Hassall and wannabe suitor, Terry Scott, in *Carry On Loving*.

MARTIN WYLDECK

At the end of the guest-star list and appearing at the very end of the episode, Martin Wyldeck made his contribution to *Fawlty Towers* in 'A Touch of Class'. Cast as the no-nonsense Sir Richard Morris, he has his patience well and truly tested when Basil bids an unorthodox farewell to the discredited Lord Melbury. Wyldeck had been a popular face on stage and television for many years, and made his mark in television situation comedy some 20 years earlier when he played Charlie Hackett in *My Wife's Sister* with Dora Bryan.

SERIES ONE

EPISODE ONE
A TOUCH OF CLASS

FIRST BROADCAST: 19 SEPTEMBER 1975

**'"A Touch of Class" was a very experimental episode
but I remember I was very pleased with the way it had gone.'**

John Cleese

I N THE first instance, 'A Touch of Class' serves to introduce us to all the main characters who make up life at 16 Elwood Avenue, Torquay.

From the outset, Cleese, as Fawlty, is bored with the day-to-day chores of management, from hanging a picture to wrestling with a typewriter as he clumsily thumps out the day's menu. Straight away we know he's not a happy man, and we soon know why. Prunella Scales as Sybil Fawlty is dominant from the beginning of the series, continually bossing around her reluctantly obedient husband, oblivious to, or uncaring of, his murderous looks and muttered sarcasm. As retaliation goes, Basil's defiant mumblings are pretty mild, and we're

left in no doubt as to who wears the trousers in this household.

John Cleese has said of Basil Fawlty that he is interested in people only if they offer him the chance of social climbing. This first episode of the series presents Basil in all his fawning and toadying glory. And, of course, the higher he tries to climb, the further he has to fall ...

Connie Booth as waitress-cum-receptionist Polly is the calming influence on Basil's seething angst, and Andrew Sachs as Manuel wanders ineffectually around the place as the hapless waiter from Barcelona, unintentionally responsible for much of the havoc building up around him.

The retired Major, played by Ballard Berkeley, is a long-term resident obsessed with the latest cricket scores and anxious only to know if the papers have arrived or if the bar is open. The twittering old ladies Miss Tibbs and Miss Gatsby make an uncredited appearance, their roles only being taken over by Gilly Flower and Renée Roberts from episode two.

Frustrated by the calibre of his guests, Basil places a £40 advertisement in

Country Life to try to attract 'a higher class of clientele' and 'turn away some of that riff-raff'. In walks leather-jacketed Danny Brown (actor Robin Ellis), whose cockney speech immediately marks him out in Basil's mind as an undesirable guest: 'Have you seen the people in room six? They've never even sat on chairs before.' Basil takes an instant dislike to him, and says that there are no rooms available – Sybil immediately gives Mr Brown room seven.

When Brown later realizes that Manuel has a poor grasp of English, he strikes up a conversation in Spanish, thereby turning Basil's dislike to hatred. (He expects Manuel to buckle down and learn English, not least because his own command of Spanish is diabolical.) At this stage, no one knows that Mr Brown is in fact an undercover police officer to whom the increasingly rude and obnoxious Basil will later be much indebted.

Meanwhile, the bogus Lord Melbury (Michael Gwynn), who is just the sort of client that Basil thinks he wants to attract to his hotel, checks in. With his smart tailoring and cultured accent, he appears to be a toff, but it is only

when he has trouble filling in his registration form that we begin to wonder about his true status. Fawlty is, as always, impatient, petulant and bordering on the downright rude. He takes a phone call while barking out instructions to his new guest until, that is, he tells Basil that he has no first name, and is known simply as 'Lord' Melbury. Basil, phone receiver by his ear, goes goggle-eyed, snaps 'Go away' to the caller (O'Reilly of the next episode) before hastily slamming the phone down and beginning his sickening ingratiation

ABOVE: 'I'm so happy! … Thank you, thank you, your lordship.'

BELOW: Lord Melbury's 'valuables'.

of the high-class stranger.

Nothing is too much trouble for Basil to ensure his noble guest's pleasure. He moves other residents around the dining room in an effort to give Melbury the best table, offers him free titbits ... Such attentions inevitably lead Melbury to concoct his plan to relieve Basil of his prized coin collection, as well as a couple of hundred pounds, all of which the excited hotel owner is more than happy to part with. When Melbury asks to cash a cheque, Basil is overjoyed, crying, 'I'm so happy', as the trickster deprives him of his hard-earned money. Rubbing shoulders with aristos is what he has always aspired to, believing that he and they appreciate the finer things in life – a touch of Brahms, for example, that has always been hastily switched off by his intolerant wife.

As John Cleese says, 'The key to Basil is the snobbery. Therefore we thought that in the first episode someone who was pretending to be a lord and who wasn't would take advantage of Basil in a particularly endearing way. And Michael Gwynn who did the part was not only excellent, he was very funny. He told me about a hotel – a lodging house – he used to stay in. They had so many signs up – do this, do that, switch the light off – that if you carried out all the commands issued by the signs, they wouldn't need any staff in the hotel at all. I always remember him saying that. It was a wonderful insight into Basil and *Fawlty Towers* in general.'

Very simply, then, the first episode establishes

the whole character of Basil Fawlty. We both laugh at and pity him from the very beginning. And when his dream of social advancement is shattered – by the realization that he has been duped by the bogus lord, whose 'valuables' deposited in the safe turn out to be bricks – we almost wish that, as he holds the objects up, shakes and sniffs them, he could salvage something from the experience. Shouting 'Bastard!' and trying to kick the fraudster as he is led away by the police are the only comforts he has. So much for attracting an upper class clientele ... His touching, but unsuccessful, attempt at thanking Manuel for his part in apprehending the rogue reveals a little-seen seed of warmth in Basil's frustrated character.

John Cleese was satisfied with the pilot: '"A Touch of Class" was a very experimental episode but I remember I was very pleased

ABOVE: 'Ow's me old mucker?' Basil finally discovers the truth about 'Lord' Melbury.

OPPOSITE TOP: 'Could somebody answer that, please? ... Not you.'

with the way it had gone. Although Connie was very happy with the overall show, she wasn't happy about a couple of the little bits with her as the philosopher. I said, "Don't worry we can redo those."' Indeed, the original script, which specified Polly as a philosophy student, was adapted. Adding a few lines of dialogue between Polly and Mr Brown about her sketches was all that was required to change Polly from a philosopher to an aspiring artist. The final version was as near perfection as he could have hoped. 'One or two of my closest friends, with whom I work well, were very pleased with it and encouraged me a lot. I felt that we were all right and that we were on to something good.'

A TOUCH OF CLASS

BASIL FAWLTY John Cleese
SYBIL FAWLTY Prunella Scales
MANUEL Andrew Sachs
POLLY Connie Booth
LORD MELBURY Michael Gwynn
DANNY BROWN Robin Ellis
MAJOR GOWEN Ballard Berkeley
SIR RICHARD MORRIS Martin Wyldeck
MR MACKENZIE David Simeon
MR WAREING Terence Conoley
MR WATSON Lionel Wheeler

Written by **JOHN CLEESE & CONNIE BOOTH**
Film Cameraman **LEN NEWSON**
Film Editor **BILL HARRIS**
Costumes **MARY WOODS**
Make-up **CHERYL WRIGHT & JEAN MCMILLAN**
Production Assistant **MIKE CRISP**
Lighting **CLIVE THOMAS**
Sound **MIKE JONES**
Music **DENNIS WILSON**
Designer **PETER KINDRED**
Produced/Directed by **JOHN HOWARD DAVIES**

EPISODE TWO
THE BUILDERS

FIRST BROADCAST: 26 SEPTEMBER 1975

**'Basil always tries to get something done on the cheap.
My father was a tiny little bit like that.'**

John Cleese

BASIL and Sybil haven't been away for a weekend since her close friend Audrey 'had her hysterectomy', so the couple are long overdue some time off, and the weekend will prove a useful opportunity to have some much-needed building work done on the hotel. Sybil, having had some bad experiences, wants to use the reputable builder Mr Stubbs. As John Cleese recalls the name was no accident: 'Connie and I used the name Mr Stubbs because we were great friends with Nicky Henson and Imogen Stubbs, and Mr Stubbs, who was Imogen's father, was actually a builder. In fact, he helped us on the show. He didn't actually play the part of the builder, but we got a lot of technical stuff about RSJs and the like. Those little bits of research are very good if you can get them right. It helps to make the comedy all that more real.'

Basil, in his endless quest to save money and prove that he is not as incompetent as his nagging wife makes out, prefers to use someone cheaper, even if that someone still hasn't finished building the garden wall he started four months ago. John Cleese sees Basil's

meanness as an integral part of the Fawlty character. 'Basil always tries to get something done on the cheap. My father was a tiny little bit like that. For instance, if my mother had asked him to buy some ham, he would always come back in and she would look at what he

ABOVE: 'Manuel Towers. How are you? Is nice today. Goodbye.'

OPPOSITE TOP: 'Oh, don't smile.' Basil shows his experience in the ways of Sybil.

OPPOSITE MIDDLE: 'You're a naughty boy, Fawlty! Don't do it again!'

OPPOSITE BOTTOM: 'She's in here with me, Basil.'

had bought and say, "This isn't the usual ham." He would say, "No, they have some special Norwegian ham this week. They recommend it very highly. They said it's better than the ordinary stuff." In reality, it was just cheaper. He would always buy pairs of shoes that looked slightly odd and would fall apart after three weeks. He was always trying to save money. In that way, Basil is very much like my father.'

Of course, Basil doesn't exactly tell his wife that Stubbs won't be doing the building work. His choice of firm is the cowboy outfit of Mr O'Reilly with its 'lick o' paint' and 'tea and biscuit' philosophy.

While the Fawltys are away Polly is left in charge of the hotel, but, overworked and in much need of some sleep, she leaves it in the more than incapable hands of her Spanish colleague, Manuel, with strict instructions to wake her when the builders arrive. Manuel enjoys lording it over the almost-empty hotel, proving himself as an able manager and promptly trying to book a garden gnome into room 16. Clearly copying his

employer's behaviour, he treats a persistent telephone caller whom he believes is asking to speak to Mr Fawlty with impatient rudeness. Almost drunk with power, he compassionately decides not to wake Polly when the builders arrive and takes charge of 'Orelly' man's crew himself. It's no surprise that, under such guidance, O'Reilly's men misread the plans and build everything back to front. The caller phones again, and this time Manuel understands that it is Basil himself, who instructs Manuel, by way of punishment for earlier rudeness, to call one of the burly builders a hideous orang-utan. The resulting punch in the face does something to appease Basil.

The Fawltys return, and Basil can't believe the builders' botch-up, but Sybil can. She had, after all, warned him repeatedly about O'Reilly. Enter the builder himself who, if he didn't believe Basil's claim before that his wife can kill a man at 10 paces with one blow of her tongue, must surely do so now. Sybil sets about him with an umbrella, her shouted insults drowning first his attempts at pacification, and then his defeated gibbering. This scene also illustrates Basil's cowardice: happy to rant and rave when he has no opposition, he cannot cope when real complaining is called for. Sybil handles it crisply and efficiently, ordering O'Reilly out and demanding Stubbs be brought in to put things right. But, Basil, like a suicidal moth, flies back towards the flame. Determined not to lose face with the infuriatingly, perpetually right Sybil, he's not going to get Stubbs: he's going to get O'Reilly to sort out his own mess, and he'll stand over him so that nothing can go wrong...

By some miracle, it seems that nothing has, and O'Reilly has done a proper job for once in his life. It is, of course, too good to last and Stubbs's expert eye reveals the fatal flaw in the workmanship. Basil is last seen leaving the hotel intent on inserting a garden gnome into the builder who has embarrassed him, once again, in front of Sybil.

Although many people consider this episode their favourite, John Cleese finds it unsatisfactory and thinks his performance was poor, though this judgment comes largely from the studio audience reaction, which was very muted. 'We performed almost entirely to complete silence. It was not a very comfortable experience. Afterwards I was disturbed and people kept saying, "No, it was a funny show," but I moaned, "What about the audience?" I found out later that a large number of people from the Icelandic Broadcasting Corporation had visited the BBC that day. The BBC, always helpful to shows like mine, thought it would be nice if they put all 70 of them in the front row. They just sat there being very pleasant and charming and

Icelandic and not laughing at all. All we got was a faint whiff of cod coming from the front row which, had we recognized it at the time, might have given us the explanation. Still, it was a tough recording and it needed quite a lot of editing to tighten it up. I still think it's the least good of the 12 shows we did.'

'I'm going to see Mr O'Reilly, dear. Then I think I might go to Canada.'

THE BUILDERS

BASIL FAWLTY John Cleese
SYBIL FAWLTY Prunella Scales
MANUEL Andrew Sachs
POLLY Connie Booth
MAJOR GOWEN Ballard Berkeley
MR O'REILLY David Kelly
MISS TIBBS Gilly Flower
MISS GATSBY Renée Roberts
MR STUBBS James Appleby
DELIVERY MAN George Lee
LURPHY Michael Cronin
JONES Michael Halsey
KERR Barney Dorman

Written by **JOHN CLEESE & CONNIE BOOTH**
Film Cameraman **STANLEY SPEEL**
Film Editor **BOB RYMER**
Costumes **MARY WOODS**
Make-up **JEAN SPEAK**
Production Assistant **TONY GUYAN**
Lighting **GEOFF SHAW**
Sound **JOHN HOWELL**
Designer **PETER KINDRED**
Produced/Directed by **JOHN HOWARD DAVIES**

EPISODE THREE
THE WEDDING PARTY

FIRST BROADCAST: 3 OCTOBER 1975

'It's always struck me that people who aren't getting enough sex
are fascinated by it and those people who get it.'
John Cleese

A WEEKEND of sultry heat and an impending wedding result in a sexually charged atmosphere at *Fawlty Towers,* which provides all the ingredients for a classic farce: two couples, friends of Polly, pop in and out of each other's rooms, with Basil wandering in at inopportune moments, people wander round skimpily clothed or in various states of undress, and Basil catches Polly passionately kissing her boyfriend across the reception desk. Everyone is a little preoccupied with sex, but none more so than Basil, as he answers the phone: 'Fawlty Titties.'

In this episode, John Cleese pinpoints a common attitude to sex: 'It's always struck me that people who aren't getting enough sex are fascinated by it and those people who get it. As often as not, that frustration takes the form of being very, very cross that other people are getting some. And that's always been Basil's problem. I mean, I'm not quite sure when he and Sybil last did it, but it's a very, very long time ago ... somewhere at the end of the Punic War I suspect. And the essence of this episode was all about how disapproving he is. He tries to catch them at it, and I enjoy very much the degree of how he gets worked up. It's that whole thing of when people say, "I'm not a prude but ...", which always means "I am a prude" of course. This episode is an exploration of all that stuff.'

Even Sybil seems to be affected by the steamy atmosphere, flirting with a hotel guest at the beginning of the episode, and letting rip with the laugh that drills right into Basil's brain. He rebuts her innuendoes about 'no nuts' in the bar with comments about the film *How To Murder Your Wife*: 'I've seen it six times, you know.' In his jealous prudishness, he refuses to allow the unmarried couple a double-bedded room, blaming his decision on 'the law of England', very pleased to allocate them two single rooms at different ends of the hotel. Sybil quickly reverses his decision, which does nothing to ease his frustration.

Innocent comments and enquiries become sexually loaded in his overheated mind. One guest wants to know if there's a chemist nearby. He needs a couple and has left his at home – perhaps Basil has some? Basil's alarmed and disgusted response is horribly embarrassing, as we know, from an earlier scene with Polly, that the guest simply wants a few batteries for his razor and not the implied condoms. When the penny finally drops with Basil, his clumsy attempts to extricate himself from the situation, as usual, make things worse.

Manuel, meanwhile, is celebrating his birthday, for which the Fawltys have given him an umbrella. He tries to read out a touching speech of thanks to his boss, but is brusquely stopped from doing so. As the day wears on, Manuel becomes drunker and his speech increasingly maudlin. This is one distraction too many for Basil, and he cruelly rips the speech to pieces, in a sad contrast to his stern attempt at sentiment at the end of the first episode.

As Manuel gets increasingly impassioned, the guests begin to detect homosexual undertones, doing little to relieve the tired and overheated Basil, already disturbed by the bewilderingly sympathetic and flirtatious Mrs Peignoir (Yvonne Gilan). She recognizes his classical music, which Sybil

always dismisses, she flatters him, she understands him, hopes that his wife 'appreciates' him, suggests that she shouldn't leave him 'with strange women', reveals that she sleeps naked ... Any lesser man would surely succumb, but Basil is more terrified than tempted. Marriage, like a murder sentence, is for life, and he's signed up for the duration.

John Cleese believes that Basil is flattered but never really interested: 'He could never handle anything actually sexual, but he quite likes going into a sort of 1920s', slightly sophisticated attitude of trying to play along with it. Of course, he'd be terrified if it actually became a reality, which is of course what happens with the French lady in this episode.

Here he has no idea how to handle it at all. But a little graceful, old-fashioned flirtation is something that he can manage quite well. In fact, when I think of it, that's probably what attracted Sybil to him in the first place.'

We even get a chance to see the sort of marital disharmony that he is trying to preserve: he lies reading *Jaws* while Sybil, in a separate bed, smokes cigarettes, scoffs chocolates and gratingly laughs at a magazine.

It is the last straw for Basil when loud groans of pleasure (actually the result of a very good massage) are heard emanating from the room of the young couple. In a one-man moral crusade, Basil orders all the guests, plus Polly, out of the hotel, seconds before being told by Sybil that

the couples are related, and good friends of Polly, and there has been no hanky-panky going on whatsoever. Sybil explains that all he has to say is that he's sorry but he's made a mistake. For Basil, life can never be that easy. The most he can manage is an oily, 'I'm so sorry, but my wife has made a mistake.' 'Yes, I think she probably did,' is the guest's reply.

Already discomfited, Basil spends the rest of the night plagued by the unwanted attentions of Mrs Peignoir. Even though Sybil is supposedly spending the night with the unhappy Audrey, Basil's terror of her extends far too far to allow him to respond to Mrs Peignoir with anything but hissed requests to 'Go to your room. I won't ask you again,' and attempts to pretend that his wife is with him in the room after all. This is unfortunate when his caller turns out to be Sybil, returned unexpectedly, and convinced there's a burglar downstairs. Only half dressed, Basil investigates,

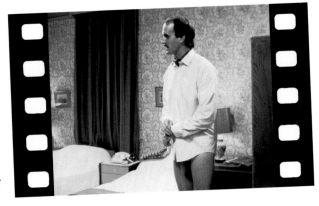

heroically felling the 'burglar' with a frying pan. The realization that he has battered the hungover Manuel has him bending over the unconscious waiter in remorse, but this quickly turns to fury, as he is once again caught in a compromising position by the thoroughly amused wedding party.

ABOVE: 'Try to control yourself. Where do you think you are? Paris?' Basil attempts to fend off Mrs Peignoir.

OPPOSITE: 'Ah, Mr Fawlty, you're so charming.'

THE WEDDING PARTY

BASIL FAWLTY John Cleese
SYBIL FAWLTY Prunella Scales
MANUEL Andrew Sachs
POLLY Connie Booth
MAJOR GOWEN Ballard Berkeley
MRS PEIGNOIR Yvonne Gilan
MR LLOYD Conrad Phillips
MRS LLOYD Diana King
ALAN Trevor Adams
JEAN April Walker
MISS TIBBS Gilly Flower
MISS GATSBY Renée Roberts
BAR GUEST Jay Neill

Written by **JOHN CLEESE & CONNIE BOOTH**
Music **DENNIS WILSON**
Costumes **MARY WOODS**
Make-up **JEAN SPEAK**
Production Assistant **TONY GUYAN**
Lighting **GEOFF SHAW**
Sound **JOHN HOWELL**
Designer **PETER KINDRED**
Produced/Directed by **JOHN HOWARD DAVIES**

EPISODE FOUR
THE HOTEL INSPECTORS

FIRST BROADCAST: 10 OCTOBER 1975

'It is not possible to reserve the BBC2 channel from the commencement of this televisual feast, until the moment of the termination of its ending, thank you so much.'

Basil Fawlty to Mr Hutchison

WE REALLY see what an awful man Basil is in this episode,' says John Cleese, 'because he has no interest at all in other human beings as human beings. They're either objects of derision and scorn or an opportunity to improve his position in the social hierarchy. In this particular case, it's the professional hierarchy. He is painfully aware that he needs a good recommendation for his hotel, and I love the idea that by having different people arriving and departing and Basil never quite knowing which one of them is the inspector we created an opportunity for the character to switch from one way of addressing a guest to another and back again without any kind of consistency. We could really see what a bastard he was.'

When Mr Hutchison (Bernard Cribbins) arrives, Basil is not aware of his guest's occupation, and vents his natural irritation at his ornate language. The question, 'Is it possible for me to reserve the BBC2 channel for the duration of this televisual feast?' is responded to in equally florid language, as Basil replies: 'It is not possible to reserve the BBC2 channel from the commencement of this televisual feast, until the moment of the termination of its ending.

LEFT: 'I wish you'd help a bit. You're always refurbishing yourself.'

OPPOSITE TOP: 'As the map is sadly inadequate I would be very grateful if you could draw me a diagram of the optimum route.'

Basil's anger has no bounds. Bad enough that his sucking-up has been wasted – but to waste it on this most troublesome guest is too much. As lunch continues, he contrives to abuse Mr Hutchison verbally and physically, almost knocking him unconscious during one tiff. Basil then turns his attention to the neglected Mr Walt, whom, he now believes, must surely be the hotel inspector. Bowing and scraping is now revived for a new recipient, until the battered Hutchison returns to wreak his revenge on Basil.

'I am not a violent man, Mr Fawlty,' Hutchison announces as he batters him quite brutally, while Basil attempts to maintain a complaisant air for the benefit of the watching Mr Walt. 'You've handled that, then, have you, Basil?' interjects Sybil. Even Basil is not able to fool himself that Hutchison's assault can be passed off as playful banter with an eccentric regular, and his belief that the incident will find its way into the report of the 'hotel inspector' leaves him a quivering, moaning wreck. The

Thank you so much.' But when Hutchison declares Basil's response a shame because he has had wide experience of hotels in his 'professional capacity', Basil completely changes his tune. For the supposed hotel inspector, the BBC2 channel is suddenly reservable, and none of his requests are too much trouble. 'Well, that's what we're here for, isn't it?' fawns Basil.

Fellow guest Mr Walt (James Cossins) observes the goings-on with Mr Hutchison with some bemusement. His own lunch is disrupted when he is moved from table to table to give preference to the supposed inspector, and insult is added to injury when the bottle of wine he is served turns out to be corked. Meanwhile, all the table changes result in people receiving the wrong meals, and everyone is vociferous in their complaints. In the midst of the confusion Sybil drops the bombshell that Mr Hutchison is a spoon salesman, not a hotel inspector.

revelation that Mr Walt actually sells outboard motors has Basil expressing some of the sincerest gratitude we ever hear from him: 'Thank you ... thank you so much ...' until his attention suddenly turns to what he is now free to do to the departing Mr Hutchison.

As Basil and Manuel see Hutchison off the premises with a custard pie in the face, Basil suddenly realizes that the three men who have just arrived and witnessed these events, must be the real inspectors. His scream of horror can be heard well beyond Torquay ...

ABOVE: Basil and Manuel help Mr Hutchison on his way.

OPPOSITE: Basil mistakes two of his guests for hotel inspectors.

THE HOTEL INSPECTORS

BASIL FAWLTY John Cleese
SYBIL FAWLTY Prunella Scales
MANUEL Andrew Sachs
POLLY Connie Booth
MR HUTCHISON Bernard Cribbins
MR WALT James Cossins
MAJOR GOWEN Ballard Berkeley
MISS TIBBS Gilly Flower
MISS GATSBY Renée Roberts
JOHN Geoffrey Morris
BRIAN Peter Brett

Written by **JOHN CLEESE & CONNIE BOOTH**
Music **DENNIS WILSON**
Costumes **MARY WOODS**
Make-up **JEAN SPEAK**
Production Assistant **TONY GUYAN**
Lighting **GEOFF SHAW**
Sound **JOHN HOWELL**
Designer **PETER KINDRED**
Produced/Directed by **JOHN HOWARD DAVIES**

EPISODE FIVE
GOURMET NIGHT

FIRST BROADCAST: 17 OCTOBER 1975

**'...it took a very long time to find a branch that was right.
We tried beating the car with a fairly rigid branch and it wasn't funny at all.'**
John Cleese

ASIL FAWLTY is still trying to rid his hotel of the riff-raff he feels it is saddled with. He wants to embrace the cream of Torquay society, and be recognized as a hotelier and restaurateur extraordinaire. That's assuming he can get the blasted car started. Sybil insists he takes it into the garage, but once again – in penny-pinching mode – Basil wants to fix it himself. John Cleese says, 'Basil is desperately trying to improve the tone of the hotel. I love the fact that he says in the advertisement "No riff-raff". He thinks, again, that with the right sort of people he can improve his professional chances and perhaps get invited to dinner with some of these people. He's at his fawning worst.'

In his bid to attract a classier guest, Basil has brought in a new Greek chef, Kurt, for the hotel's gourmet night. The chef's cooking is superb and he's getting on well with Manuel and Polly – even buying a sketch of Manuel from Polly 'for money'.

If ever Basil needed further justification for holding a *haute cuisine* evening at his hotel, the spoilt brat complaining about the shape of his chips while his doting parents look on provides it. He controls his temper as these 'proles' demand salad cream instead of the freshly made mayonnaise – 'That's puke that is' declares the child. 'Well, at least it's fresh puke,' retorts Basil.

The big night arrives, the regular guests and residents are packed off for the evening and Basil, in full dinner suit, prepares for the highlight of his hotel career. When Sybil breaks the news that four of the guests have cancelled at the last minute, the venom spews out once again. He's rough and gruff with his elderly regulars, but then velvety smooth at the arrival of Colonel Hall and his diminutive wife (Allan Cuthbertson and Ann Way). He is

equally fawning to the Twitchens (Richard Caldicot and Betty Huntley-Wright).

But trouble is brewing. Kurt has a crush on Manuel, but Manuel tells him 'no cuddle'. The devastated chef turns to the bottle for comfort. Polly tries to let her boss know that the chef is drunk, without giving the game away to the on-looking guests, but Basil is too wrapped up in his 'high society' guests to listen. Polly finally confronts him with the bad news, and he is greeted in the kitchen by the spurned Greek, hopelessly drunk and conspicuously failing to cook the special menu. Basil and the chef wrestle before the chef collapses, paralytic. Overcoming hysteria, Basil makes a quick call to pal André at his high-street restaurant. The evening can still be salvaged as long as the guests like duck – duck with orange, duck with cherries or duck surprise ('that's duck without orange or cherries'). After Mrs Hall is half-poisoned by uncooked mullet hors d'oeuvres, Basil drives off to get the main course.

Cleverly avoiding the expected gag of the car not working, Basil makes the journey and brings the prepared duck back to the hotel. Unfortunately, the bird gets trodden on, so Basil's off on the second emergency dash of the evening. This time the car does stall *en route*. Maddened beyond endurance, Basil wrenches off the branch of a tree and beats the car with it. John Cleese remembers the difficulty of

getting the scene right: '... it took a very long time to find a branch that was right. We tried beating the car with a fairly rigid branch and it wasn't funny at all. We tried beating it with a floppy branch and that didn't work. Then we finally got a branch that had the right degree of flexibility and it became terribly funny. It showed that no matter how good an idea is, there's always an enormous amount to getting it right technically. Nobody realizes unless they actually do it. Similarly, when Basil's cursing

OPPOSITE: 'When you're presenting *haute cuisine*, you don't want the working class sticking its nose in it.'

RIGHT: Visiting chef Kurt drinks too much and passes out after his advances to Manuel are turned down.

inside the car, the sound is contained as though it's coming from inside a goldfish bowl, which makes it much funnier. If the audience heard it at full volume from inside the car, it would lose a lot of its comic power.'

While Basil is suffering car problems, Polly and Manuel are trying to keep the increasingly hungry guests amused with dancing and song, followed by Sybil's risqué tales of her Uncle Ted. Basil, running all the way in his desperation to save his dreams of culinary fame, finally makes it back to proudly present his guests with … a large trifle. Rummaging around the gelatinous mass, he finally musters the words 'Duck's off. Sorry!'

John Cleese considers the final sequence of 'Gourmet Night' as the best he has ever written, but is aware that even the best plots can be improved upon: 'Shortly after the episode was transmitted I went to a very good restaurant in Cambridge, and they'd had a similar emergency on their first night. They'd been cooking and had friends in attendance trying out trial meals. On the night in question the gas company cut off the gas. In the excitement and frenzy of opening the restaurant, they'd quite simply forgotten to pay the bill. That was a neater way of getting to the stage where you don't have any way of cooking the meal properly and you have to go to the restaurant down the town. That was much better than the one we came up with.'

OPPOSITE: 'Right! That's it! You've tried it on just once too often! … Well this is it! I'm going to give you a damn good thrashing!'

GOURMET NIGHT

BASIL FAWLTY John Cleese
SYBIL FAWLTY Prunella Scales
MANUEL Andrew Sachs
POLLY Connie Booth
ANDRE André Maranne
KURT Steve Plytas
COLONEL HALL Allan Cuthbertson
MRS HALL Ann Way
MR TWITCHEN Richard Caldicot
MRS TWITCHEN Betty Huntley-Wright
MAJOR GOWEN Ballard Berkeley
MISS TIBBS Gilly Flower
MISS GATSBY Renée Roberts
MR HEATH Jeffrey Segal
MRS HEATH Elizabeth Benson
MASTER HEATH Tony Page

Written by **JOHN CLEESE & CONNIE BOOTH**
Music **DENNIS WILSON**
Film Cameraman **STANLEY SPEEL**
Film Editor **BOB RYMER**
Costumes **MARY WOODS**
Make-up **JEAN SPEAK**
Production Assistant **TONY GUYAN**
Lighting **RON KOPLICK**
Sound **JOHN HOWELL**
Designer **PETER KINDRED**
Produced/Directed by
JOHN HOWARD DAVIES

EPISODE SIX
THE GERMANS

FIRST BROADCAST: 24 OCTOBER 1975

**'Don't mention the war … I mentioned it once, but I think
I got away with it all right …'**
Basil to Polly

Ask anyone who's watched *Fawlty Towers* which episode they recall more than any other and most will nominate 'The Germans', usually followed by cries of 'Don't mention the war!' and visions of Basil strutting around like a deranged Pythonesque Nazi. John Cleese, however, has reservations about the show. 'I never think the second half of 'The Germans' is as well written as all that. There are several things in it that I think are wrong, whereas I think the first half of it is written beautifully. I've always been fascinated by people trying to communicate and not being able to – Michael Palin's stuttering scene in *A Fish Called Wanda* is a favourite, and the fire drill sequence here works in the same way. It's a situation when two people are trying to understand each other and just missing each other's meaning. I don't know why I find it so funny, but I always do. The fact that he's trying to explain to his guests that it is not the fire alarm but the burglar alarm is just an opportunity for that sort of comedy. I love the moment where Basil gives up and says, "I don't know why we bother anyway … we should let you all burn." I love that line.'

LEFT: 'I'm actually about to undergo an operation, Basil.' Sybil prepares for open-toe surgery.

OPPOSITE TOP: The Major explains his philosophy of women and cricket to Basil.

OPPOSITE MIDDLE: 'You see, I speak English well, I learn it from a book. Hhhello.'

OPPOSITE BOTTOM: *'Fuego, fuego, fuego.* Mr Fawlty! Is fire!'

me to do what I'm already doing? I mean what is the bloody point? I'm doing it, aren't I?' She hears of further chaos, including Basil jamming himself under the reception desk, and getting hit on the head by a vase of flowers, from an unperturbed Polly.

We get a brief glimpse into the Major's past in this episode, as Basil's disparaging remarks about Sybil draw out the confession, 'Strange creatures, women ... I knew one once'. We gather, however, that though he took the girl in question to see India – at the Oval – nothing came of his brief moment of romance, as the ungrateful thing ran off with his wallet, and was never seen again. The Major returns to the lobby minutes later to be greeted by the spectacle of a talking moose (actually a hidden Manuel practising his English while he cleans under the counter). 'I can speak English. I learn it from a book,' the moose intones, while the Major takes it better than most might, merely commenting to Basil, 'A remarkable animal ... Japanese, was it?'

The episode opens with Sybil in hospital on the eve of surgery for an ingrowing toenail. This should leave Basil completely in charge of the hotel, but Sybil haunts him even from her sickbed, making her presence felt via the telephone. His first task – hanging a moose head on the wall – makes him increasingly irascible, especially as Sybil constantly interrupts proceedings. 'I was just doing it, you stupid woman! I just put it down to come here to be reminded by you to do what I'm already doing! I mean, what's the point of reminding

As Basil tries to get on with the other task Sybil set him – going through the six-monthly fire drill – he unwittingly sets off the burglar alarm. The guests assemble for Fire Drill, and Basil tries to explain to the assembled guests that this isn't the actual fire drill – the fire bell

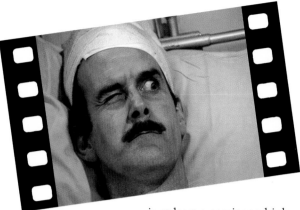

is at least a semitone higher than the alarm bell, and they'll have to go through the drill again. Meanwhile, told to make chips to get him out of the way, Manuel actually does set fire to the kitchen, but his cries of 'Fire' are ignored, as both Basil and Polly believe he is just being, as ever, slow on the uptake. Finally managing to get his message across, he staggers smoking around the lobby, eventually knocking Basil out with his frying pan as the unfortunate proprietor wrestles with a fire extinguisher.

The concussion Basil suffers leads to a short stay in hospital, where he is greeted by his wife, who neatly sums up his catalogue of failures so far. 'Polly cannot cope!' he announces. 'Well,' replies Sybil, 'she can't fall over waiters, or get herself jammed under desks, or start burglar alarms, or lock people in burning rooms, or fire fire extinguishers straight in her own face. But I should think the hotel can do without that sort of coping for a couple of days, what do you think, Basil, hmmm?' Undeterred, Basil discharges himself early, and with a deranged look of cunning returns to the hotel with his head bandaged and even less ability than

usual to control his words and actions. To be met by the Germans.

John Cleese explains, 'The point I was trying to make with the German sequence is that people like Basil are utterly stuck in the past. If you look at the episode, all the people that he was interacting with are much too young to have had anything to do with the Second World War. [Most of us can] let it go. Basil can't do that.'

From the first, Basil is not quite himself, as his guests' efforts to make themselves understood are met by the less then helpful 'Oh, German! I thought there was something wrong with you.' He then, in his efforts not to mention the war, proceeds to bring it into conversation at every available juncture, causing particular upset for one of the women of the party.

Although Basil's behaviour is clearly the result of his concussion, his German guests are obviously offended by his rants. The more ordinary and vulnerable they appear to be the more outlandish and insulting Basil's antics become. In reference to their current con-versation, the elder German maintains, 'We did not start it.' Basil, still ranting about the past, shouts, 'Yes you did, you invaded Poland.' His

looser-than-usual grasp on the acceptable, caused by the blows to his head, allows him to voice unconscious attitudes that even Basil, in his normal state, might see as irrational.

Cleese exercises tight control over the pace of the episode's climax, as he gradually increases the speed of his character's tirade, so that the final seconds, during which he makes little or no attempt to hide his blind distaste for his guests, are delivered at breakneck speed. This, and the out of the blue bigotry, 'You stupid Kraut,' and 'Who won the bloody war, anyway?' show us a character fascinatingly and frighteningly close to the edge of rationality.

The episode ends as Basil's doctor arrives to apprehend him and get him back to hospital where he clearly belongs. With manic guile, Basil leads the doctor on a chase round the hotel, which culminates in Basil being felled by the falling moose head, which then lands on Manuel's head as he is still recovering from a blow from Basil. 'Oh, he hit me on the head,' he moans, but the Major is not fooled. 'No, you hit him on the head. You naughty moose!' he says, giving the culprit a rap on the nose. 'However did they win?' one of the Germans sighs.

Perhaps surprisingly, the episode was well-received in Germany. Indeed, one of Cleese's fondest memories followed its screening in Germany: 'I was in Hamburg ... and as I walked across the lobby of my favourite hotel, a German voice shouted out to me, "Hey, Mr Cleese, don't mention zee war!" I thought that was terrific. It's taken a little time, but I felt really good about that. That chap had got the whole point of the episode.'

THE GERMANS

BASIL FAWLTY John Cleese	Written by **JOHN CLEESE & CONNIE BOOTH**
SYBIL FAWLTY Prunella Scales	Music **DENNIS WILSON**
MANUEL Andrew Sachs	Film Cameraman **STANLEY SPEEL**
POLLY Connie Booth	Film Editor **BOB RYMER**
MAJOR GOWEN Ballard Berkeley	Costumes **MARY WOODS**
MRS WILSON Claire Davenport	Make-up **JEAN SPEAK**
MISS TIBBS Gilly Flower	Production Assistant **TONY GUYAN**
MISS GATSBY Renée Roberts	Visual Effects **PETER PEGRUM & KEN BOMPHRAY**
SISTER Brenda Cowling	Lighting **RON KOPLICK**
DOCTOR Louis Mahoney	Sound **JOHN HOWELL**
MR SHARP John Lawrence	Designer **PETER KINDRED**
MRS SHARP Iris Fry	Produced/Directed by **JOHN HOWARD DAVIES**
GERMAN GUESTS Willy Bowman	
Nick Kane	
Lisa Bergmayr	
Dan Gillan	

SERIES TWO

WATERY
FOWLS

EPISODE ONE
COMMUNICATION PROBLEMS

FIRST BROADCAST: 19 FEBRUARY 1979

'I was fascinated with the idea of getting a slightly complicated episode together
in which a whole series of stories depended on each other.'

John Cleese

TAKE the simple device of a continually complaining guest with hearing problems, and combine it with Basil, desperate to keep a secret from his domineering spouse, and you have the makings of a classic episode.

One of *Fawlty Towers'* most popular one-off characterizations was Mrs Richards (excellently played by Joan Sanderson). She was inspired by a holiday encounter, as John Cleese explains: 'Connie and I were in Monte Carlo for two weeks and we met a very nice woman who was helping us at the hotel. We had coffee with her and said, "What's the most difficult kind of guest that you have?" We were researching even on holiday you see! Anyway, this lady described Mrs Richards absolutely perfectly. We wrote it all down and what we had was the complete character portrait: the fact that they always complained about everything but they didn't want anything changed, they just wanted a reduction. And this brilliant business of strategic

deafness, hearing just what they want to hear and nothing else. The character couldn't fail.'

It's St George's Day – a special day for Basil Fawlty, because it celebrates the man who killed a hideous, fire-breathing dragon. 'Why did he kill it?' asks the Major, 'I don't know, Major,' replies Basil, 'Better than marrying it.'

Mrs Richards is not happy with her room, and Basil is unsympathetic. She's paying £7.20 a night, plus VAT, and the bath's not big enough to drown a mouse. ('Wish you were a mouse.') More to the point, the view of Torquay isn't good enough, which prompts another sarcastic reply from Basil. Still the room is unsatisfactory because the radio doesn't work. ('No, the radio works. You don't.') Despite her complaints, Mrs Richards decides to stay. In an effort to make life easier for them all, Basil offers to have her hearing aid fixed. There's nothing wrong with it, she insists; she keeps it off to save the battery!

Saving money is the underlying theme of the episode. Mrs Richards is a miser, uttering her complaints simply to get a reduction on her stay at the hotel, and playing on her ageing, hard-of-hearing persona for all it's worth. However, the equally penny-pinching Basil is also looking to find ways to make himself some extra cash.

In order to build this element into the story, John Cleese was happy to embrace a vintage plot device and a perennial human addiction: 'I was fascinated with the idea of getting a slightly complicated episode together in which a whole series of stories depended on each other. The idea was that if one collapsed, all the others collapsed. For some reason we hit upon betting,

which is not a very strong taboo. In fact, it's probably the weakest of the taboos, but there's a Pinero play about a vicar who puts money on a horse and spends the entire two and a half hours trying to cover up the fact. Well, of course, nowadays you'd say, why bother?'

Many people, of course, consider this episode one of the finest comedy half-hours

ABOVE: 'Ooh, I know … I know … ooh, I know.'

OPPOSITE: A combination of a hard-of-hearing, cantankerous old lady, a waiter from Barcelona and an irascible hotelier lead to considerable 'Communication Problems'.

ever shown on television, but Cleese isn't convinced: 'In a way, the fact that it's no big deal gambling behind your wife's back explains why this is not one of the very best episodes. Still, all the tensions between the characters work and the comedy builds up very nicely.' (And, after all, while gambling behind your wife's back may be no big deal, when your wife is Sybil Fawlty, you may have reason to be a little worried.)

The episode boasts the rare sight of a satisfied customer – 'Perhaps we should have him stuffed,' quips Basil. When that same guest imparts a red hot betting tip within earshot of Sybil, Basil pretends to be completely uninterested, even aping Mrs Richards' deafness to hammer the point home. Without Sybil's knowledge, Basil is going to get a bet on the sure-fire nag if it kills him.

Meanwhile, Mrs Richards' demands lead to further misunderstanding. Her request for toilet paper in room 22 is misinterpreted by Manuel, who delivers her 22 rolls.

Basil couldn't care less though. His horse has just come in and he has won wads of unaccounted cash. As long as Manuel doesn't spill the beans, Sybil will never find out. Things start to go wrong when Mrs Richards reports that she's had £85 stolen from under her mattress. Still Basil doesn't care. Somewhat power-crazed by his new-found riches, he is callous about Mrs Richards' loss, even reck-lessly incurring the wrath of Sybil. In a poignant moment, Basil takes Sybil's hand, and says, 'Do you remember, when we were first manacled together, we used to laugh quite a lot?' Removing his hand, she replies, 'Yes, but not at the same time, Basil.'

The usually hard-up Polly, whom Basil briefly entrusts with his winnings, is earlier spotted with the cash and is now interrogated by Sybil. Making it up as she goes along – not a good idea when talking to Sybil – Polly insists she overheard a racing tip and gambled on the horse herself. 'Polly, what was the name of the horse?' demands Sybil, and behind her, Basil transforms himself into a manic parody of Marcel Marceau in a frantic attempt to mime the name of the horse. Polly makes several wild guesses (with Basil pointing at Sybil as a clue) – Bird Brain, Fish Wife and Flying Tart, before eventually arriving at Dragonfly. Sybil is not fooled: 'If I find out the money on that horse was yours, you know what I'll do, Basil.' 'You'll have to sew 'em back on first,' comes the bitter reply.

ABOVE: 'Three o'clock. Exeter. Dragonfly.'

OPPOSITE: Basil recovering in the office after a particularly savage attack from Sybil.

John Cleese in rehearsal for one of the final scenes where Basil thinks he's finally come out on top.

Desperate to keep the money away from his wife, Basil hides it with the Major, who subsequently forgets the whole conversation. His memory returns and he produces the cash just as Sybil turns up. She thinks it's the missing loot of Mrs Richards, and with heavy heart, Basil has to hand his winnings to the uncomprehending guest from hell. The Major's memory goes again, so Basil desperately turns to Manuel to corroborate his story. Manuel remembers the instruction given earlier and proudly declares 'I know nothing' over and over again. With barely contained rage, Basil opens the till with his head then offers to give Mrs Richards the shirt off his back.

Basil's chagrin turns to joy when a local shopkeeper delivers a vase bought by the deaf old lady and returns the money she left by mistake in her glove at his shop. Basil grasps it for dear life: 'For the first time in my life I'm ahead! I'm winning!' he cries. Sadly, his joy is short-lived. He only has a deliciously self-centred moment, as Mrs Richards asks whose money Basil has and he wickedly intones: 'This is mine!' before Sybil finds out the money discovered earlier was Basil's winnings after all, and sheer unadulterated panic sets in. When Mrs Richards' vase gets smashed in the ensuing debacle, Basil is forced once more to hand over his money.

John Cleese is particularly proud of the closing scene: '... when they're all standing in a line and all the lies are beginning to collapse one after another. Suddenly, the lies kind of start to get built up again. I like that section very much. I think any time I see a possibility of a misunderstanding, I jump on it. It's one of my two or three favourite kinds of humour.'

COMMUNICATION PROBLEMS

BASIL FAWLTY John Cleese
SYBIL FAWLTY Prunella Scales
MANUEL Andrew Sachs
POLLY Connie Booth
MRS RICHARDS Joan Sanderson
MAJOR GOWEN Ballard Berkeley
TERRY Brian Hall
MISS TIBBS Gilly Flower
MISS GATSBY Renée Roberts
MR THURSTON Robert Lankesheer
MR FIRKINS Johnny Shannon
MR MACKINTOSH Bill Bradley
MR KERR George Lee
MR YARDLEY Mervyn Pascoe

Written by **JOHN CLEESE & CONNIE BOOTH**
Music **DENNIS WILSON**
Costumes **CAROLINE MAXWELL**
Make-up **SUZAN BROAD**
Lighting **RON BRISTOW**
Sound **MIKE JONES**
Videotape Editor **HOWARD DELL**
Production Assistant **JOHN KILBY**
Design **NIGEL CURZON**
Producer **DOUGLAS ARGENT**
Director **BOB SPIERS**

EPISODE TWO
THE PSYCHIATRIST

FIRST BROADCAST: 26 FEBRUARY 1979

'This episode is all about Basil's dislike of any kind of sexual behaviour.'
John Cleese

LIKE 'The Wedding Party' in Series One, 'The Psychiatrist' derives much of its humour from Basil Fawlty's fear of sexual activity. The guests on this occasion include a couple of doctors – one of whom turns out to be a psychiatrist – a bronzed male who fancies himself as a bit of a love god and a pretty Australian blonde. From the moment they arrive you know that Basil and his prudishness won't stand a chance.

It's a typical morning at the seaside hotel. Sybil is drawling 'I know' on one phone while on another, Basil is hassling the operator, wanting to know why the speaking clock is engaged. In walks the self-confident Mr Johnson (Nicky Henson), charming any woman who cares to listen. He even flirts with Sybil, who finds the attention most welcome and energetically flirts back, much to the mounting unease and annoyance of Johnson himself. Basil is put out: 'You seem to think that we girls should be aroused by people like Gladstone, Earl Haig and Baden Powell,' Sybil surmises. She then skewers Basil's declared hatred of male decoration (in the form of Johnson's random collection of gold medallions) by pointing out that he doesn't object to his military heroes decorating themselves with medals. Basil, although adamant that it's not the same, is silenced by this argument.

John Cleese says: 'This episode is all about Basil's dislike of any kind of sexual behaviour. There are some very good lines at the beginning about how people dress, and as Sybil says, Basil's

ABOVE: Basil on the warpath, determined to expose the loose morals of the younger generation.

OPPOSITE: Basil undermines his own efforts to convince the psychiatrist of his sanity.

idea of a sexy, attractive man is Earl Haig. She cleverly points out that he did actually wear his decorations. It's quite an interesting line because she's right. Basil doesn't mind his heroes wearing decoration when it involved killing people and the army. All these brightly coloured things are exactly the same as the trinkets the Nicky Henson character wears really.'

When the Abbotts arrive, and Basil discovers they are both doctors, he greets them with much fawning and jolly banter. At this stage, however, he is unaware that one is a psychiatrist and might be judging his behaviour with a professional eye. When the Abbotts have gone to their room, Basil seeks revenge on Sybil for her flirtatious behaviour with Mr Johnson by complimenting Mrs Abbott:

BASIL: 'That outfit that Mrs Abbott is wearing, you should get yourself something like that.'

SYBIL: 'What, for the gardening, you mean?'

BASIL: 'Attractive woman. How old would you say she was?'

SYBIL : '48, 50.'

BASIL: 'Oh, no, Sybil.'

SYBIL : 'I really don't know, Basil. Perhaps she's 12.'

Feeling that he's won this spat, Basil proudly leaves the reception area with further wisecracks implying that the open-shirted Mr Johnson has hardly made the evolutionary step up from the apes.

Having upset his wife and believing himself now to have just the quality of guest he wants in the hotel, Basil approaches dinner with more enthusiasm than usual. He strikes up a friendly conversation with the Abbotts, keen to impress them with the fact that he too once contemplated becoming a surgeon, but Sybil slaps him down: 'A tree surgeon … had to give it up. Couldn't stand the sight of sap.' When Mrs Abbott reveals that she is a paediatrician, Basil again tries to impress, but succeeds only in showing his ignorance: 'Feet,' he blurts. 'Children,' she replies. To counter Sybil's exasperation he defiantly asks, 'Well, children have feet, don't they?' doing little to dig his way out of the hole.

Then comes the bombshell: Mr Abbott announces that he's a psychiatrist. Basil immediately becomes agitated, certain that his

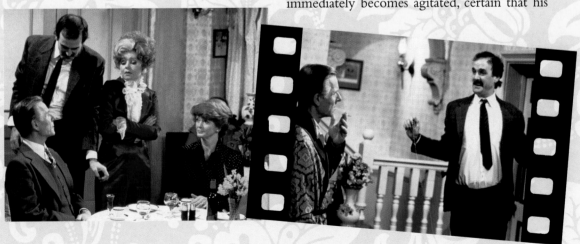

every move is being judged. Sybil tries to calm him down by insisting that the Abbotts are at the hotel to get away from it all. He's unappeased: 'You know what they say it's all about, don't you? Sex. Everything's connected with sex. What a load of cobblers …' Basil, now riddled with self-doubt, doesn't hear the Abbotts wondering how the Fawltys manage a holiday but snaps out of his reverie when he hears them ask how often he and Sybil 'manage it' – once or twice a year? Mrs Abbott doesn't think they can 'manage it' at all. Basil is infuriated and proudly announces that they manage it at least two or three times a week. By the time he realizes that they are talking about holidays rather than sex, he is beyond rescue: his paranoia has been revealed in full.

John Cleese maintains: 'That scene is the key to the episode. It's all about Basil's utter embarrassment about any kind of talk of emotions, and his ill-informed assumptions about what psychotherapy is about. Maybe, I've been lucky with therapists – you can have good and bad ones, like you can have good or bad plumbers or doctors – but Basil seems to go along with the British press attitude that analysis should be attacked. Stupidly, it's always attacked for being what it isn't. But it makes people anxious. On the whole, people do not want to look at themselves. Most are pretty uncomfortable about it, and the presence of the psychiatrist brings out all Basil's fears … Somebody might actually start looking into what's going on inside his head. Terrifying!'

At reception Australian Raylene Miles (Luan Peters) checks in. Basil is rather taken with her, and his embarrassment at Sybil's noticing this provides cover as Mr Johnson smuggles his girlfriend past reception and up to his room. Basil, meanwhile, can't do enough for the attractive blonde guest, falling over himself to carry her bags upstairs and helpfully fixing a light in her bathroom. When, reaching round into the bedroom, he grasps her breast rather than the light switch, Sybil inopportunely witnesses it, and is coldly dismissive: 'One word of advice. If you're going to grope a girl, have the gallantry to stay in the room with her while you're doing it.'

Basil, hearing a female laugh emanating from Johnson's room, becomes obsessed with proving the existence of the clandestine guest. As

'There's enough material there for an entire conference.' Dr Abbott's conclusion following Basil's alarming behaviour.

Manuel explains to Sybil, 'He try to see in room to see girl, she make him crazy,' – not helping Basil's shaky standing with his wife at all.

The incriminating implications build up as Sybil keeps catching her husband in compromising positions with Raylene, and Basil ends up forbidden from the conjugal bedroom for the night. The physical comedy builds up with Fawlty dropping champagne bottles, tapping on walls, falling off ladders, climbing into cupboards and smearing Miss Miles's chest with black paint. His elaborate ploys to catch Johnson in flagrante backfire, and Basil succeeds only in demonstrating to the doctors that his own mental state is far from stable.

By the end of the show it hardly matters whether he was right or not. Johnson's got the girl out of his room and installed his elderly mother, forcing Basil to turn his self-righteous triumph at uncovering loose sexual behaviour

into a grovelling speech of welcome. Of course, Sybil thinks her husband's just been making excuses for chasing a young blonde, while the psychiatrist has clearly discovered that if ever a person needed some help, then Fawlty is the man.

THE PSYCHIATRIST

BASIL FAWLTY John Cleese	Written by **JOHN CLEESE & CONNIE BOOTH**
SYBIL FAWLTY Prunella Scales	Music **DENNIS WILSON**
MANUEL Andrew Sachs	Costume **CAROLINE MAXWELL**
POLLY Connie Booth	Make-up **SUZAN BROAD**
MR JOHNSON Nicky Henson	Film Cameraman **ALEC CURTIS**
DR ABBOTT Basil Henson	Film Sound **BILL CHESNEAU**
MRS ABBOTT Elspet Gray	Film Editor **SUSAN IMRIE**
MAJOR GOWEN Ballard Berkeley	Studio Lighting **RON BRISTOW**
TERRY Brian Hall	Studio Sound **MIKE JONES**
RAYLENE MILES Luan Peters	Videotape Editor **NEIL PITTAWAY**
MRS JOHNSON Aimee Delamain	Production Assistant **JOHN KILBY**
MISS TIBBS Gilly Flower	Design **NIGEL CURZON**
MISS GATSBY Renee Roberts	Producer **DOUGLAS ARGENT**
JOHNSON'S GIRLFRIEND Imogen Bickford-Smith	Director **BOB SPIERS**

EPISODE THREE
WALDORF SALAD

FIRST BROADCAST: 5 MARCH 1979

'The whole point about 'Waldorf Salad' is that the Americans can do what the English can't. The English can't complain.'
John Cleese

ON THE night of a huge storm, the Fawltys prepare to welcome their first transatlantic guests to the 'English Riviera'. In the dining room Sybil is chatting to a guest at great length, explaining just how busy life can be when running a hotel, while Basil demonstrates the truth of her words, frantically rushing around the restaurant, grudgingly serving customers and being vehemently rude to those who complain.

John Cleese firmly believes that 'the English don't know how to complain. We're so over-polite in a lot of situations – it's almost like a neurosis. I can remember sitting at a lunch table in Los Angeles once and I saw an Englishman up

the other end and he wanted the salt. Instead of saying, "Could you pass the salt?" he just sat there for about seven or eight minutes until somebody looked at him and he pointed to it and said, "Sorry". That was his way of asking for the salt. We're terribly apologetic. I like the fact that some Americans are capable of being very direct in a way that achieves the object without ever seeming rude. They can just assert themselves with the right degree of energy.

'The whole point about "Waldorf Salad" is that the Americans can do what the English can't. The English can't complain because we think it's going to be aggressive and something to do with losing your temper and losing face. When Basil goes up and asks two old dears if their meal is all right they reply, "Oh yes, very nice thank you." Seconds earlier they had been complaining [between themselves] about the poor quality of the food.'

Indeed, most of the guests at *Fawlty Towers* don't answer back ... except Mr and Mrs Johnston

(Terence Conoley and June Ellis) who aren't happy with their hors d'oeuvres and have eaten most of them just to make sure: '... Oh, deduct it from the bill, is that what you mean?' asks Basil. 'As it's inedible.' 'Only half of it's inedible apparently.' 'Well, deduct half now, and if my wife brings the other half up during the night, we'll claim the balance in the morning.'

The Arrads (Norman Bird and Stella Tanner) are cheesed off too. Manuel has been getting their order wrong and the dominant wife tells her henpecked husband to complain. Basil's response is to turn the complaint around: 'You only have to eat here. We have to live with it. I had to pay his fare all the way from Barcelona. But you can't get the staff, you see.' Mrs Arrad looks incredulously at her husband: 'You were supposed to be complaining to him.'

A glamorous middle-aged woman, Mrs Hamilton (Claire Nielson), arrives. Suddenly, Basil is charm itself, describing her room with its panoramic view of the garden in glowing terms. While his back is turned a loud American (Bruce Boa) walks in complaining about the dreadful weather and the size of British motorways. Basil is irritated by the criticism, particularly in front of such a sophisticated woman: 'Well, I'm sorry it wasn't wide enough for you. A lot of the English cars have steering wheels.' He continues to insult the man until Mrs Hamilton introduces him as her husband.

The drenched guests want dinner, but it's after 9 p.m. and the restaurant is closed. The American is irate: 'What the hell's wrong with this country? You can't get a drink after three, you can't eat after nine, is the war still on?' Basil

explains it's the staff. Offered £20 to keep the staff on to make them dinner, Basil accepts, but he can't persuade anyone to stay: Terry the chef has got a 'karate' lesson with a tall blonde Finnish woman, and Manuel is going out with Polly. Basil will have to look after the guests himself.

Almost immediately, the cultural differences start to cause problems. The Hamiltons each want a screwdriver: 'Nothing to drink?' Basil asks. The couple settle on vodka and orange instead. While Basil prepares the drinks in the kitchen, Sybil does rather a good job of engaging the Americans in conversation. Basil returns from the kitchen with the drinks, and things turn frosty again. He attempts to defend the British weather, and declares, to far from rapturous response, that they have palm trees in Torquay.

When the Hamiltons announce they would like a Waldorf salad, Basil looks momentarily blank, then declares, 'I think we're just out of Waldorfs.' He knows that, in taking over the catering for the evening, he's out of his depth, but he's damned if he's going to admit it and suggests they try a Ritz salad of apples, grapefruit and potatoes in a mayonnaise sauce instead. They aren't interested in his imaginary concoction or the ridiculous excuses he tries to fob them off with, and Hamilton instructs him to go and bust the chef's ass. 'Bust his …?' 'Ass!' While Fawlty threatens to break his chef's 'bottom', Sybil delivers the salads. Mr Hamilton catches Basil 'arguing' with the 'chef' for all he is worth, and his patience snaps for

the umpteenth time that night. He berates Basil and his hotel roundly.

With complete confidence, Basil, choosing as his supporters the guests who he knows are too scared to disagree, eloquently defends both his hotel and his country in the face of this American attack. Unperturbed, Mr Hamilton seizes upon a lone dissenting voice, and encourages the guests to tell Basil how they really feel. Stunned, his retort is surely just the kind of invective that every hotelier would applaud: 'You ponce in here expecting to be waited on hand and foot, well I'm trying to run a hotel here.' Basil tells his wife that either the guests leave or he does. Inevitably, it's Basil who goes and soon he's out in the very British weather he had earlier seemed so keen to defend.

TOP: Mr Hamilton lays in to Basil after being offered a Ritz salad of apples, grapefruit and potatoes in a mayonnaise sauce.

OPPOSITE: 'What I'm suggesting is that this is the crummiest, shoddiest, worst-run hotel in the whole of Western Europe.'

WALDORF SALAD

BASIL FAWLTY John Cleese
SYBIL FAWLTY Prunella Scales
MANUEL Andrew Sachs
POLLY Connie Booth
MR HAMILTON Bruce Boa
MRS HAMILTON Claire Nielson
MR ARRAD Norman Bird
MRS ARRAD Stella Tanner
MR JOHNSTON Terence Conoley
MRS JOHNSTON June Ellis
TERRY Brian Hall
MR LIBSON Anthony Dawes
MAJOR GOWEN Ballard Berkeley
MISS TIBBS Gilly Flower
MISS GATSBY Renée Roberts
MISS GURKE Beatrice Shaw
MISS HARE Dorothy Frere

Written by **JOHN CLEESE & CONNIE BOOTH**
Music **DENNIS WILSON**
Costume **VALERIE SPOONER**
Make-up **SUZAN BROAD**
Lighting **RON BRISTOW**
Sound **MIKE JONES**
Videotape Editor **NEIL PITTAWAY**
Production Assistant **JOHN KILBY**
Design **NIGEL CURZON**
Producer **DOUGLAS ARGENT**
Director **BOB SPIERS**

EPISODE FOUR
THE KIPPER AND THE CORPSE

FIRST BROADCAST: 12 MARCH 1979

**'If the guest isn't singing "Oh What a Beautiful Morning"
I don't immediately think, "Oh there's another one snuffed it in the night."'**
Basil Fawlty

IT'S every hotel owner's nightmare – a guest dying on the premises. Most would deal with it by quietly calling for an ambulance and the police and making as little fuss as possible. Not Basil Fawlty. He, instead, fails to notice that his guest has died, even though their breakfast conversation is very one-sided.

John Cleese recalls how the episode was inspired: 'A restaurateur by the name of Andrew Leeman was a great friend of mine and one day I asked him, "What's the worst problem you had when you used to work at the Savoy Hotel?" Quite straight-faced he replied, "oh, the stiffs." I said, "the what?" and he continued, "getting rid of the stiffs. The old dears knew the Savoy would always treat them really well, so they would check in with a bottle of pills, take them in the night, and in the morning the Savoy staff would walk in, pick up the phone and say, 'We've got another one.' Then the problem was getting the stiffs into the service elevator without alarming the other guests." Well, I mean to say, once you've been given that as an idea, it's just wonderful. And then you put a doctor in the hotel and it's a kind of a joy.

Those ideas just write themselves. In fact, we called the dead body Mr Leeman in Andrew's honour.'

The episode starts relatively peacefully in the bar. Mrs Chase (Mavis Pugh) is showing off her little dog, Prince, to the Major (Ballard Berkeley). 'He's a little Chitzu.' 'Really?' he says. 'What breed is it?' Fellow guest Dr Price (Geoffrey Palmer) has missed his dinner and rather fancies some sausages. A ham sandwich is all Sybil can offer, and she volunteers Basil to go and make it.

Looking rather ill and pale, Mr Leeman (Derek Royle) picks up his key to room 8. Sybil is kindness itself to her poorly guest, but Basil mistakes illness for laziness. When the guest requests breakfast in his room, Basil demands: 'Is it your legs? Most of our guests manage to struggle down in the morning.' Basil continues: 'If you can remember to sleep with your mouth open you won't even have to wake up. I'll just drop in small pieces of lightly buttered kipper when you're breathing in the right direction, if that doesn't put you out.'

The next morning Dr Price is still yearning

for sausages and Mrs Chase's shih-tzu is causing a stir in the dining room. After badgering Sybil and Terry the cook about the kippers being past their use-by date, Basil takes breakfast up to Mr Leeman, delivering a diatribe about the state of the country, socialism and strikes, as he opens the curtains. The guest doesn't say a word, which Basil interprets as more rudeness from an unappreciative guest. It's only when Polly takes up the milk, which had been left off the breakfast tray, that the dreadful truth emerges. He's dead. 'Well, that would explain a lot,' is Basil's first reaction. Then he remembers the out-of-date kippers, and all hell breaks loose. The kippers have to be retrieved, even though Polly points out that the guest has been dead for hours. Dr Price arrives and wants to know why, if Leeman was dead when Basil delivered the breakfast, Polly had returned with the milk. 'You mean to tell me you didn't realize this man was dead?' asks the doctor. 'Well, I'm just delivering a tray, right? If the guest isn't singing "Oh What a Beautiful Morning" I don't immediately think, "Oh there's another one snuffed it in the night. Another name in the *Fawlty Towers* Book of Remembrance."'

John Cleese was continually trying to stretch the emotions of his character: 'I was fascinated by the idea of trying to get Basil very happy about the fact someone had died. We came up with the idea that he thought he'd poisoned him, and then when he discovered that he hadn't poisoned him, he'd be really happy. At

Basil and Manuel now have two bodies to deal with: the dead guest, Mr Leeman, and unconscious resident Miss Tibbs.

that moment the doctor could walk in and catch Basil screaming with joy. It's that utter, ruthless selfishness again. No thought for this poor guy or his family at all. It's just that he's off the hook.'

With the kippers in the clear, the only problem remaining is how to get the body off the premises without any of the other guests finding out. While Mr Leeman is being moved from one end of the hotel to another, elderly Miss Tibbs literally stumbles on the truth, and in an effort to calm her hysterics, Polly slaps her a little too hard, knocking her out. 'Oh, spiffing,' shouts Basil, 'Two dead, only another 25 to go!' They take both 'bodies' into the nearest room, just as the guests occupying it return to pick up their things before a day out. Mr White (played by Welsh actor Richard Davies) becomes increasingly irate as Basil tries to prevent him and his wife from entering the room. When they eventually get in, they find a hysterical Miss Tibbs in their cupboard.

The dead body is moved down to the office, where the Major finds it, but is not overly perturbed. 'Shot, was he?' 'No, no, no. Died in his sleep.' 'Ah, well, you're off your guard, you see!'

Dr Price is still waiting for his sausages while a recomposed Miss Tibbs goes to the office to complain about her earlier treatment. Encountering the body again, she passes out.

The body is then moved to the kitchen, where the doctor, impatient for his sausages, discovers it. He's outraged. 'Wash your hands first, please. And make sure this area is scrubbed before any more food is prepared in here. Sausages excepted. You may cook them immediately. I'll take the risk.'

In the meantime, Mr Leeman's friends arrive to pick him up. Basil assumes they're from the undertakers and takes them to the linen basket – the corpse's latest resting place – only to find that it's been collected by the laundry. One sprint down the front steps later, the basket, with Leeman, is returned. The body does another trip round the hotel alerting almost every guest to what has happened and in the process bringing everyone together in the reception for the macabre climax to the show. Manuel resigns his post and takes refuge in the laundry basket. With nowhere left for Basil to hide the body, the game is up and Mr Leeman is now in full view for everyone to see. Basil escapes the madness he has created by having the laundry picked up again – with him in it. Only the Major is oblivious to it all, calmly tapping the seated corpse on the shoulder and asking, 'What's going on, old boy?'

John Cleese reveals that the ending could have been funnier if he had been brave enough to make it a lot darker: 'We thought it would be terribly funny if we established the existence of a twin brother without Basil knowing. So the plan was that after Basil had finally got the stiff in the basket, the twin brother would walk in and come up to the desk. Basil would abuse him over this mindless practical joke he had played, but we couldn't do it because there was no way of Basil telling the twin that his

OPPOSITE: Basil finally comes clean to Mr Leeman's colleagues, only to discover that the body is on the way to the laundry.

RIGHT: Basil offers to post Mr Zebedee's hat to him to save him losing it in the high winds.

brother was dead. You couldn't do that in a comedy show, but it was a great shame. It would have been hilarious but we couldn't have mixed that kind of emotion. I think we got the balance between laughs and the macabre just about right. I love bodies in baskets!'

THE KIPPER AND THE CORPSE

BASIL FAWLTY John Cleese
SYBIL FAWLTY Prunella Scales
MANUEL Andrew Sachs
POLLY Connie Booth
DR PRICE Geoffrey Palmer
MRS CHASE Mavis Pugh
MR WHITE Richard Davies
MRS WHITE Elizabeth Benson
MAJOR GOWEN Ballard Berkeley
MISS TIBBS Gilly Flower
MISS GATSBY Renée Roberts
TERRY Brian Hall
MR LEEMAN Derek Royle
MR XERXES Robert McBain
MISS YOUNG Pamela Buchner
MR ZEBEDEE Raymond Mason
MR INGRAMS Charles McKeown
GUEST Len Marten

Written by **JOHN CLEESE & CONNIE BOOTH**
Music **DENNIS WILSON**
Costume **CAROLINE MAXWELL**
Make-up **SUZAN BROAD**
Film Cameraman **ALEC CURTIS**
Film Sound **BILL CHESNEAU**
Film Editor **SUSAN IMRIE**
Studio Lighting **RON BRISTOW**
Studio Sound **MIKE JONES**
Videotape Editor **HOWARD DELL**
Production Assistant **JOHN KILBY**
Design **NIGEL CURZON**
Producer **DOUGLAS ARGENT**
Director **BOB SPIERS**

EPISODE FIVE
THE ANNIVERSARY

FIRST BROADCAST: 19 MARCH 1979

'I think it's one of the very best episodes.'
John Cleese

SOMETHING'S amiss at *Fawlty Towers*. Sybil is allowing her 'sensitive nature' to get the better of her as she thinks Basil has forgotten their 15th wedding anniversary. Basil,

meanwhile, is whistling 'Ode to Joy' and appearing to be very happy indeed. It's obvious from the start that he hasn't forgotten, and is planning a surprise celebration.

Basil has promised to lend Polly £100 for a new car, but he keeps fobbing her off now that the time has come to hand over the cash. Chef Terry is up in arms when he hears that Manuel is to cook an anniversary paella in his kitchen. 'I have been to catering school,' he protests. While all this is happening, Basil fails to spot his distraught spouse leaving the premises in a fit of pique.

As Sybil departs, the guests for the surprise party start to arrive. Now, of course, he could just tell the truth about Sybil's absence, everybody would have a good laugh and the show would be over in about four minutes. But Basil's perpetual feeling that he has something to hide comes to the fore, and he begins to weave a web of excuses that becomes ever more elaborate under the close questioning of his friends. 'What am I going to say?' he asks Manuel in desperation. 'Is surprise party ... She not here ... that is surprise!' Manuel suggests.

After his plan to make Sybil fume backfires, Basil is left in the lurch with a hotel full of expectant party guests.

Smart-alec friend Roger (Ken Campbell) realizes that all is not well almost immediately, but doesn't let on, instead choosing to point out Basil's every inconsistency as he digs himself deeper into the mire. Handed his drink, Roger sarcastically says: 'Up yours, Bas.'

As more guests arrive and are told that Sybil is unwell, they want to know why the doctor hasn't been to see her. Polly and Basil conspire to keep the subterfuge going, mishearing commands so that's Sybil's alleged ailments appear to have spread from puffiness of the thighs to puffiness of the eyes. Friend Virginia, a nurse, is worried by this, and demands to see Sybil. The situation can only deteriorate, as the last batch of friends arrives with the news that they've just seen Sybil driving through the town: 'That's the other woman ... that woman

who looks slightly like Sybil,' Basil blusters, scraping the very bottom of the barrel.

The friends point out they have come to see the happy couple and are terribly disappointed that Sybil's not there. 'I'm sorry if you've been put out,' says Basil. 'You have some drinks, plenty of nuts, see your old friends, have a few laughs, but if that isn't good enough, I'll refund your petrol for you.' When they guests appear even more suspicious, he challenges anyone who thinks he's a liar to go upstairs and visit his poorly spouse. The guests are embarrassed, though Roger seems rather keen.

So it's up to Polly: she'll have to stand in as the missing wife: 'But I don't look like her!' 'You're a woman aren't you?' Basil retorts, which explains a lot about the success of his marriage. Basil pretending to collapse of a heart attack doesn't melt Polly's heart. Only the offer of £100 for her car does. The guests convene outside Sybil's bedroom door, and they are eventually allowed into the darkened room, where they can just make out a Sybil-like figure. While they try to make conversation with the 'patient', the real Sybil makes a surprise return. Basil, too embarrassed to tell her what's happened, offends her with his offhand manner and she promptly leaves again – much to his relief.

Following Polly's attack on the nurse Virginia, hitting the concerned friend when she tries to get too close for comfort, the shocked guests get ready to leave, just as Sybil

ABOVE: 'Syb-ill. Bas-well. Ha ha!'

RIGHT: 'Look! Look! It's perfectly Sybil! Simple's not well. She lost her throat and her voice hurt.'

reappears in reception. Basil, accusing her of being the Sybil double he invented earlier, bundles her into a cupboard as the guests leave. Congratulating himself on his cleverness, he mutters, 'Piece of cake ... Now comes the tricky bit.' The rest is left to be all-too-easily imagined by the audience.

John Cleese is proud of this episode: 'Basil is actually thinking of someone else for a short period of time before the panic overtakes him. And you do get the impression that there is something positive underneath all the other stuff between him and Sybil. Connie and I particularly like that episode because we felt that we were beginning to explore character a bit more. It was a little less farcical than usual. I remember we thought it was in the area of Alan Ayckbourn, who we both adored.'

Industrial action also gave the cast and crew more opportunity to get the show right: 'Because of a BBC strike, we had extra time to rehearse ... It was really good because everyone was able to get familiar with the show and then bring little things to it. Also the extra time allowed us to unintentionally think up lots of visual business. We didn't add any dialogue because when that was good, you didn't need any more. But you got more and more chance to work out visual gags which ran parallel with the dialogue and simply made the mix richer. I think it's one of the very best episodes.'

THE ANNIVERSARY

BASIL FAWLTY John Cleese	Written by **JOHN CLEESE & CONNIE BOOTH**
SYBIL FAWLTY Prunella Scales	Music **DENNIS WILSON**
MANUEL Andrew Sachs	Costume **CAROLINE MAXWELL**
POLLY Connie Booth	Make-up **SUZAN BROAD**
ROGER Ken Campbell	Film Cameraman **PAUL WHEELER**
ALICE Una Stubbs	Film Sound **BILL CHESNEAU**
ARTHUR Robert Arnold	Film Editor **SUSAN IMRIE**
VIRGINIA Pat Keen	Studio Lighting **RON BRISTOW**
REG Roger Hume	Studio Sound **MIKE JONES**
KITTY Denyse Alexander	Videotape Editor **HOWARD DELL**
AUDREY Christine Shaw	Production Team **JOHN KILBY**
MAJOR GOWEN Ballard Berkeley	**PENNY THOMPSON**
MISS TIBBS Gilly Flower	**IAIN MCLEAN**
MISS GATSBY Renée Roberts	Design **NIGEL CURZON**
TERRY Brian Hall	Producer **DOUGLAS ARGENT**
	Director **BOB SPIERS**

EPISODE SIX
BASIL THE RAT

FIRST BROADCAST: 25 OCTOBER 1979

'Don't you have rats in Spain, or did Franco have them all shot?'

Basil Fawlty

IT'S fitting that the last episode of *Fawlty Towers* is generally considered one of the very best. Owing to a TV strike in 1979, viewers watching the series the first time round had to wait seven months before this episode was finally transmitted. There's no doubt, however, that it was worth the wait.

Sybil is having a go at Basil, who in turn has a go at the first person he sees – a man on his knees examining the hotel's kitchen fridge.

He's the local health inspector (drily played by John Quarmby), who proceeds to read out a list of faults which silences everyone except Terry: 'Filthy Towers', he quips.

Meanwhile, Manuel is in his room playing the guitar to his pet – a genuine filigree Siberian hamster, also known as a common or garden rat. A sympathetic Polly explains to the disconsolate waiter that he's been slightly misled as to the animal's true identity.

Downstairs, Sybil is rattling off a list of things Basil must do to remove the health hazards in the kitchen. 'Can't we get you on *Mastermind*, Sybil? Next contestant Sybil Fawlty from Torquay, special subject the bleeding obvious.'

Of course, the rat must go, but in a rare soft-hearted moment, Sybil suggests that Basil should try to find it a good home: 'All right! I'll put an ad in the papers! "Wanted, kind home for enormous savage rodent. Answers to the name of Sybil."'

Sybil suggests having it put to 'S.L.E.E.P.' and while Manuel

OPPOSITE: 'Look, I'll go and get you a chair and then you can really tuck in.'

BELOW: 'Have you ever heard of the bubonic plague, Manuel? It was very popular here at one time. A lot of pedigree hamsters came over on ships from Siberia ...'

endearingly misunderstands what the word spells Basil is keen to know whether it would be cheaper to get the rat and Manuel done at the same time.

John Cleese has great affection for this episode: 'There are some very good lines early on. I love it when Manuel thinks that it's

a filigree Siberian hamster and Basil persuades him it's a rat. He says, "Don't you have rats in Spain, or did Franco have them all shot?" That's one of my favourite lines.'

The next day the hotel is spick-and-span and everyone is ready for the inspector's return. Manuel is in mourning, and wearing a black armband to prove it. Basil tries to cheer him up: 'Manuel ... my wife informs me that you're depressed. Let me tell you something. Depression is a very bad thing. It's like a virus. If you don't stamp on it it spreads throughout the mind, and then one day you wake up in the morning, and you can't face life any more.' 'And then,' Sybil sighs, 'You open a hotel.'

The depression is, in fact, all an act. Manuel has actually hidden the rat in one of the out-houses, and it's during one of his visits to his pet that we discover Manuel has named the rodent after his beloved boss. The episode gathers pace when the rat gets out and finds its way back into the hotel. Polly and Manuel try to find the rodent Basil without the human Basil noticing. When the human Basil realizes who the rodent Basil is and what's happened to his namesake, all hell breaks loose.

A trap is laid in the form of rat poison on a veal fillet. The poisoned veal then gets mixed up with the other poison-free fillets, and no one's sure if it's ended up on a guest's dinner

LEFT AND BELOW: Basil's initial sympathy for the 'loss' of Manuel's rat quickly turns into frustration causing Manuel to plead: 'Don't hit me. Always you hit me.'

ABOVE AND RIGHT: The Major takes drastic action to try to rid the hotel of pests.

plate … As the inspector arrives, the Major fires his shotgun at the rat, while Polly chases it with a huge butterfly net.

The show reaches its climax as the inspector unbelievably gives the hotel a clean bill of health. Even more surprisingly, he demands a veal lunch – it looks like the health inspector could leave the establishment with anything but a clean bill of health himself.

It all builds up to that instantly recognizable scene where the inspector is handed a tin of biscuits to go with his order of dessert cheese. The lid is dramatically lifted off the biscuit tin

to reveal Basil the rat staring at the incredulous inspector.

It's all been too much for his human namesake, who collapses. He's dragged away and with him the series and the show both come to an end.

John Cleese says: 'I'm very pleased with "Basil the Rat". There's a particular scene at the end when Basil and Manuel are talking to a young couple and they're really not taking in anything the young couple are saying. They're just trying to see where the rat is. I thought it was extraordinarily funny. I love the denouement, when we finally get Polly presenting the box of biscuits with the rat looking at the inspector and Basil actually says,

"Would you care for a rat?" I mean, what else do you say in those circumstances? And the actor John Quarmby, playing the inspector, was so good. He just looks at the rat and absolutely doesn't believe it. He knows it can't be there, although he can see it. He plays that so well. I'm very, very fond of the episode and it was a fitting farewell for Basil.'

BASIL THE RAT

BASIL FAWLTY John Cleese
SYBIL FAWLTY Prunella Scales
MANUEL Andrew Sachs
POLLY Connie Booth
MR CARNEGIE John Quarmby
MAJOR GOWEN Ballard Berkeley
TERRY Brian Hall
MISS TIBBS Gilly Flower
MISS GATSBY Renée Roberts
RONALD David Neville
QUENTINA Sabina Franklyn
MR TAYLOR James Taylor
MRS TAYLOR Melody Lang
GUEST Stuart Sherwin

Written by **JOHN CLEESE & CONNIE BOOTH**
Music **DENNIS WILSON**
Costume **CAROLINE MAXWELL**
Make-up **PAM MEAGER**
Film Cameraman **PAUL WHEELER**
Film Sound **BILL CHESNEAU**
Film Editor **SUSAN IMRIE**
Studio Lighting **RON BRISTOW**
Studio Sound **MIKE JONES**
Videotape Editor **HOWARD DELL**
Vision Mixer **BILL MORTON**
Production Team **JOHN KILBY**
    PENNY THOMPSON
    IAIN MCLEAN
Design **NIGEL CURZON**
Producer **DOUGLAS ARGENT**
Director **BOB SPIERS**

FURTHER LISTENING, VIEWING AND READING

DVD

Fawlty Towers Complete Series 1 (BBCDVD 1064)

Fawlty Towers Complete Series 2 (BBCDVD 1065)

Fawlty Towers Box Set (BBCDVD 1072)

RECORDS

Fawlty Towers (BBC Records, REB 377)

Fawlty Towers: Second Sitting (BBC Records, REB 405)

Fawlty Towers: At Your Service (BBC Records, REB 449)

VIDEO

Fawlty Towers: 'Basil the Rat' with 'Communication Problems'
and 'The Anniversary' (BBCV 6632)

Fawlty Towers: 'The Psychiatrist' with 'The Builders'
and 'The Wedding Party' (BBCV 6633)

Fawlty Towers: 'The Kipper and the Corpse' with 'Waldorf Salad'
and 'Gourmet Night' (BBCV 6634)

Fawlty Towers: 'The Germans' and 'The Hotel Inspectors'
and 'A Touch of Class' (BBCV 6635)

The Complete *Fawlty Towers* (BBCV 6636)

AUDIO COLLECTION

Fawlty Towers: Vol.1 (Audio Cassette 0563 552433)

Fawlty Towers: Vol.2 (Audio Cassette 0563 552484)

Fawlty Towers: Vol.3 (Audio Cassette 0563 552530)

The Fawlty Towers Collection: (Audio Cassette 0563 553111)

Fawlty Towers: Vol.1 (CD 0563 478187)

RECOMMENDED READING)

The Monty Python Encyclopedia by Robert Ross (B.T. Batsford, 1996)

From Fringe to Flying Circus by Roger Wilmut (Eyre Methuen, 1980)

The Complete Fawlty Towers (Scripts, John Cleese and Connie Booth) (Methuen, 1998)